"*Good Works* offers a profound paradigm for ministry whereby work with those at the margins is only 'good' to the extent that our own character and relationships with God and others are good. Turning the usual metrics upside down with refreshing power, *Good Works* illuminates the profound difference between ministry and social service agency."

– Chris Rice
coauthor, with Emmanuel Katongole, of *Reconciling All Things: A Christian Vision for Justice, Peace and Healing*

"Regardless of one's ministry context, this book about Good Works, Inc., will spiritually challenge yet profoundly reward anyone earnestly seeking to embody Christian hospitality. This account of Keith Wasserman's forty years of leadership, articulated and arranged by Christine Pohl's rich and warm theological mind, displays in the most concrete of terms what it takes to truly receive, and be received by, the other as a gift."

– Michael Gulker
president of The Colossian Forum

"As theorists and practitioners of Christ's radical hospitality, Keith Wasserman and Christine Pohl draw on their years of experience writing about and living in community to animate the relationship between good works, hospitality, and God's justice-making mission. This is crucial reading for pastors, organizers, and all who desire to build 'heroic communities' of God's peace on earth."

– Drew J. Strait
assistant professor of New Testament and Christian origins at Anabaptist Mennonite Biblical Seminary

"*Good Works* is an inspiring and beautiful book full of wisdom. It weaves together Christine Pohl's decades of insightful scholarship with the practical, lived wisdom of Keith Wasserman and the community of Good Works, Inc. This book helps us all go deeper into Jesus's call to hospitality and faithful discipleship and to be inspired to live more faithfully ourselves."

— **L. Gregory Jones**
president of Belmont University

"Wasserman and Pohl invite us to pull up a seat at the table of friendship where laughter and tears flow freely and where people who are counted as little in the eyes of the world discover they are seen and known. *Good Works* welcomes us into their home and introduces us to a family where all are embraced."

— **Michael Mather**
author of *Having Nothing, Possessing Everything:*
Finding Abundant Communities in Unexpected Places

"As a pastor in Chicago, I have heard of Good Works for years. Without hoopla, fame, or a megachurch behind them, this community of Jesus just does the work of the gospel. Keith Wasserman has followed God's invitation to live in community with those closest to God's heart: the poor, the lonely, the homeless, and the forgotten. Doing so has made Wasserman one of the richest men alive. Let his experience and teaching serve as your own invitation to a life rich in good works, alive with the goodness of God, and awake to the gifts of each day."

— **Laura Sumner Truax**
coauthor, with Amalya Campbell, of
Love Let Go: Radical Generosity for the Real World

Good Works

Hospitality and Faithful Discipleship

Keith Wasserman
Christine D. Pohl

WILLIAM B. EERDMANS PUBLISHING COMPANY
GRAND RAPIDS, MICHIGAN

Wm. B. Eerdmans Publishing Co.
4035 Park East Court SE, Grand Rapids, Michigan 49546
www.eerdmans.com

Published 2021
Printed in the United States of America

27 26 25 24 23 22 21   1 2 3 4 5 6 7

ISBN 978-0-8028-7701-7

Library of Congress Cataloging-in-Publication Data

Names: Wasserman, Keith, 1958– author. | Pohl, Christine D.,
    author.
Title: Good works : hospitality and faithful discipleship / Keith
    Wasserman, Christine D. Pohl.
Description: Grand Rapids, Michigan : William B. Eerdmans Pub-
    lishing Company, 2021. | Includes bibliographical references
    and index. | Summary: "A book about Christian mission,
    hospitality, and discipleship within local community, with
    insights drawn from Good Works, Inc., a ministry in rural
    southeastern Ohio"–Provided by publisher.
Identifiers: LCCN 2020056102 | ISBN 9780802877017 (paperback)
Subjects: LCSH: Good Works, Inc. (Athens, Ohio) | Church
    work–United States. | Christian life–United States. | Wor-
    ship. | Hospitality–Religious aspects–Christianity. | Christian
    communities–Ohio–Athens.
Classification: LCC BV4403 .W37 2021 |
    DDC 261.8/30977197–dc23
LC record available at https://lccn.loc.gov/2020056102

Unless otherwise noted, biblical quotations are taken from
The Holy Bible: Today's New International Version.

Contents

Acknowledgments

From Keith: Each of us is shaped by the friends in our lives and by the communities of people that surround us. The community of Good Works—staff, volunteers, board members, supporters, and guests—has shaped my life, thinking, and initiatives for more than forty years. Words fall very short in expressing my deep gratitude for the friendships and godly influences that have contributed to my theology, practices, and, ultimately, this book.

Over the years, individual staff members helped to write and refine the key documents of Good Works, including "Vision of Hope," and we have incorporated some of those materials directly into the book. Although their insights have often been used anonymously, I am deeply grateful for their wise and crucial contributions.

I am so very grateful for my wife Darlene, who has walked with me in risky and innovative ways of loving people since before Good Works was established. Her companionship and steadiness have brought enormous stability into my life, enabling me to become the person that I am. She also became a major help to Christine and me during the season of the final book edits. I am also grateful for the immeasurable contribution to my life from our son Timothy, who has shaped me as a follower of Jesus more than he will ever know.

Finally, I am deeply grateful to Christine. Without her friendship, encouragement, and perseverance, this book would not have been written.

From Christine: I am very grateful to the current and former staff members of Good Works and for the gifts they have brought into my life—gifts of friendship, practical wisdom, and exemplary faithfulness. Their influence on my thinking and writing has been very significant. In particular, Keith and Darlene have been precious friends and models of hospitality and generosity. I am thankful for the privilege of helping to share their insights with a broader community.

From both of us: We invited a number of former staff and board members to respond to a draft of the book and to share their comments in writing and in a Zoom call. We are so grateful for the ways they improved the manuscript. Special thanks to Andrew Bissell, Frances Garrett Bissell, Cory Blackwell, Emily Axe Blackwell, Abigail Carter Fields, Patrick Filipiak, Craig Garrison, Mark Leeman, Chris Linscott, Seth Lundeen, George Pickens, and Todd Tatum for their work. We deeply appreciate others from outside the community of Good Works who also read and responded to the manuscript: Louise Harding, Dorothy Pohl, Ron Pohl, Dylan Pohl, and Julie Tennent.

Heartfelt thanks to Asbury Theological Seminary and its community for the ways it has influenced and sustained both of our lives. The numerous sabbaticals Keith was able to spend at Asbury allowed for the years of conversation between Christine and Keith that ultimately resulted in the collaboration for this book.

Thanks also to the folks at Wm. B. Eerdmans Publishing Company, and especially to James Ernest and Jenny Hoffman. We are grateful!

Introduction

There is a hunger in the church today for local expressions of Christian life and discipleship that are authentic, rich in worship, concerned about justice, and committed to the healing and wholeness of all involved. Important insights into this life have been generated as Christians minister in community with one another and with people challenged by poverty or homelessness. The staff and volunteers of Good Works, Inc., have been working together for decades to "connect people from all walks of life with people in poverty so that the Kingdom of God can be experienced."[1] They have discovered and lived out, albeit imperfectly, a powerful expression of Christian life in its beauty and vulnerability. Wisdom from their experiences is deeply rooted in the biblical tradition and relevant to the hunger for truthful discipleship today.

This is a book about being followers of Jesus in the twenty-first century. Although a first impression of Good Works' ministry is that it is with people living on the margins, that is only one of its key dynamics. Life at Good Works is about discipleship and mission in the context of thoughtful attention to all sorts of relationships. As one longtime staff member explained, "at the center of

---

1. Good Works' mission statement. See http://good-works.net.

everything we do is the formation of relationships—relationships that can be transformative to everyone involved."

What makes this book a little different from the many others offering reflection and guidance on Christian discipleship and mission is the perspective from which it is written. For forty years, Keith Wasserman has been leading a community that ministers with people who are living in poverty or are without homes in a rural context.[2]

Doing anything for that long demonstrates a remarkable level of commitment and tenacity, but ministering continuously *in community* among people struggling with various forms of poverty also opens up a variety of insights into Christian faithfulness that are truly life changing. Wisdom from the Good Works community isn't only for folks on the edges of the church; their insights can also instruct those of us located in more conventional settings. All of us can benefit from the particular combination of integrity, intentionality, and innovation they've shown in embodying Christian practices and in attending to interpersonal relationships.

Some readers will find new ideas and challenging concepts in the book, others might respond that their commitments and practices have been confirmed and reinforced. But hopefully,

2. Recognizing that some terms, while familiar, also carry connotations that are often derogatory or inaccurate, years ago Good Works chose to describe some of the people they work alongside as "people without homes" rather than as "homeless people." Because the common cultural images of those who are "homeless" do not adequately capture the life experience of many people who have lost their homes, we will work in this book to reduce the use of the more common wording. This care with how language is used to elevate or dehumanize persons has shaped Good Works' documents and practices and sensitized many in the community to how harm can be done through the words we use to describe persons and circumstances.

everyone—whether leaders or staff in social ministries, pastors or congregation members in churches, or teachers and students in colleges or seminaries—will find the community's testimony to God's faithfulness to be thought-provoking, reassuring, and challenging.

Often, when the experience of a community or movement is described in a book, it is a snapshot or still picture of something that is actually very fluid. Condensing decades of faithfulness, mistakes, and wisdom into book chapters obscures some of the organic and messy character of life together. Those who have been part of Good Works over time will be the first to say that it isn't perfect, but it is transformative.

Good Works, Inc., is located in Athens County, within the Appalachian region of Southeast Ohio. The county includes much natural beauty, a major university, and the highest poverty rate in the state. The location is significant as it embodies some of the challenges and contradictions of human resilience, resourcefulness, and hope along with systemic poverty, neglect, and exploitation. In Central Appalachia, a region that includes much of Southeast Ohio, West Virginia, Eastern Kentucky, and Southwest Virginia, long-term challenges of underemployment, out-migration, poor public transportation, and inadequate housing and health care are combined with beautiful landscapes, deep attachment to family roots, an abiding sense of place, and rich cultural commitments.

The rural location of Good Works might suggest that its experiences with people facing poverty or loss of homes is fundamentally different from experiences of urban poverty. In some ways that is true, as many of the people who come to Good Works for assistance or support are local, largely Caucasian, and longtime residents of the area. However, issues of employment, transportation, family breakdown, domestic violence, inadequate supplies of decent housing, and addictions are similar. Also similar are some of the challenges that churches, nonprofits, and social service agencies face in providing respectful, long-term support for persons desiring a more stable environment for themselves and their children.

The Good Works community operates within the city of Athens and on its outskirts; the Timothy House is its primary shelter, while many of the gatherings and activities also take place at its more rural Luhrig Road property. Good Works is currently in the process of building a new house, Sign of HOPE, in town to welcome additional individuals who have disabilities and families facing housing crises. For decades, the Timothy House has been the only shelter for people without homes in eight counties.

The community of Good Works is made up of paid staff, interns, volunteers, residents, participants, and supporters. Staff members are both single and married. While mostly middle to lower-middle class, they come from a diverse mix of ethnic, regional, socioeconomic, and educational backgrounds. Some have experienced homelessness themselves. Staff living arrangements are varied: some live with their families, a few live on the Good Works property, others share apartments, and others live on their own. Some have been with Good Works for over twenty years, many for more than five. Men and women share leadership roles. Numbers have varied over the decades; there are generally between eighteen and twenty-five full-time and part-time staff members, and between ten and twenty interns. Over the course of a year, there are approximately 1,100 volunteers, some coming each week; others come from distant states to volunteer for a week or weekend.

Staff members are intentional about cultivating a personal relationship with Christ and work hard to preserve the unity of the body of Christ. They share a passion to love people. Interns come from many backgrounds: some are college or seminary students or AmeriCorps members; others are taking a gap year before or after college. Volunteers come from a broad range of faith commitments; they come on their own, or with church or campus groups.[3]

Over the years, certain emphases have emerged from their life together, and the book is organized around these themes. The first is the community's unrelenting focus on worship. For the staff of Good Works, worship is at the heart of discipleship, service, and community. Worship undergirds and explains their ministry. It varies in style and setting, but being worshipers is central to their identity and their life together. Every action, every relationship, every commitment is an offering given back to the God who made and loves us.

Second is their emphasis on integrity. Keith often says that Good Works' program is integrity, and their identity is worship. Integrity and worship are inseparable because the God we worship is both good and holy. A strong commitment to integrity means that *how* they do what they do is crucial. Not every choice takes them down the most efficient route, and not every strategy is shaped by concerns about maximizing an investment. But every choice, policy, and relationship is shaped by questions about whether Jesus is honored, whether the kingdom of God is reflected, and whether individuals are respected.

Perspective is the third emphasis—gaining perspective, keeping perspective, and sharing perspective. Whether it is seeking God's perspective, seeing homelessness from the perspective of being without a home, or helping staff members regain perspective after a particularly difficult encounter, perspective is crucial.

---

3. A demographic description of the people facing poverty or without homes who are welcomed by Good Works can be found in chapter 3, at the end of the section "Taking Seriously God's Perspective." See p. 83.

Understandings and commitments are fundamentally shaped by what we allow ourselves to see and experience, where we locate ourselves, and which sets of lenses we use to gain clarity of vision. Thinking about the good news of Jesus from the perspective of people who are poor or overlooked opens fresh insight into the gospel and why it matters.

A fourth emphasis is the importance of friendship and the power of sharing our social lives. Forming relationships with people who are different from ourselves allows us to understand God's kingdom in fresh ways, rearranges our assumptions, and challenges us to a more mature discipleship. When friendships flourish among people who are very different from one another, dimensions of the kingdom of God are experienced and the witness is powerful. A fresh picture of what it means to be the church or the body of Christ emerges when people have opportunities to serve and care for one another.

After several decades of guiding a community, attending to the character of faithful yet adaptable Christian leadership becomes more and more pressing. As Good Works experiences transitions in leadership, questions about sustainability, vision, and roles take on heightened significance. And this is the fifth emphasis—a concern not just for Good Works but also for any Christian organization or ministry seeking to shape leadership in a way that is Christlike and life-giving. In contrast to management models that have sometimes distorted Christian priorities, reflections on leadership from within community can offer the church some important guidance and correctives.

The concluding chapter explores the formative power of good works and the character of good or heroic communities. It reflects on how hospitality came to be the most comprehensive descriptor of Good Works' form of mission and mutuality and considers some of the holy tensions that make Good Works and good works so generative.[4] Whether expressed in community gardens, home repair, or preparing meals, the opportunity to work together for good and for the well-being of another person provides exceptional soil for growth in holiness and wholeness. Doing good works together has also turned out to be a fruitful place to partner with folks who do not identify themselves as Christians but desire to serve others. Good works are transformational for all when they are done in partnership and when partnerships are characterized by trust, integrity, and good communication.

At the end of each chapter is a series of questions that are provided to prompt further individual reflection or group discussion. The various contexts for mission and ministry at Good Works are described in the appendix.

So how is it that a small community in the middle of rural southeastern Ohio, led by a man who readily acknowledges how unlikely his life's trajectory has been, can offer wisdom for contemporary followers of Christ? One answer would be that God works in very mysterious ways, and surely that is the case. Another is that the folks at Good Works have been working intentionally to build a faithful community for a long time. They have, in a sense, practiced their way into faithfulness, integrity, mission, and discipleship. God has been faithful to them and has allowed the ministry to flourish and to bring life-giving help to thousands of people. They have wisdom worth sharing.

In their vision statement, Good Works explains their understanding of purpose:

---

4. To avoid confusion between good works as a practice and Good Works as an organization, it is important to note that the name of the organization will always be capitalized. The potential confusion, however, is also a grace-filled expression of the identity of the community.

The essence of our vision is quite simple: that we may receive the love of Jesus so deeply into our lives that it propels us to love God and our neighbors with all of ourselves, thus sharing the good news of Jesus with each person who is among us. We love God by personally growing in our obedience to Christ, and by being a faithful worshipping community. We love others by caring for and instilling hope in the vulnerable people who have been entrusted to us: those who are homeless, children who are experiencing the risks of poverty, and older adults who need physical assistance and support. We share the good news by expressing our faith in Jesus' power to transform us.

All along, we are creating ways for the body of Christ and those who do not identify themselves as Christians to partner with us for the purpose of deepening or exploring a relationship with God. Our sights are set on the revealing of God's eternal reign, in all its goodness, beauty and majesty. What we do emerges from who we are—may we be the body of Christ in the world, for the world, for the glory of God![5]

I have known Keith Wasserman since 1989. He was an auditor in the first ethics class I taught at Asbury Theological Seminary, and I have been learning from him since that first morning he joined the course. He has returned to Asbury almost every year to lecture and meet with students. Over the decades, I have had a chance to interact with him on themes of hospitality, community, moral leadership, and social justice so many times that our thinking is wonderfully intertwined. His insights have been very important to my teaching and writing, and he helped to shape several of my books, especially *Living into Community*. I've

5. "Vision of Hope," 2. See http://good-works.net/wp-content/uploads/PDF%20Documents/Vision-of-Hope.pdf.

become convinced that the wisdom he has gleaned from ministry with the Good Works community needs to be available more broadly than what can be shared in a few classes, on the Good Works' website, or on his speaking circuit. For me, Good Works has been a "demonstration plot"[6]—not because it is perfect but because it embodies so many of the best impulses of Christian community, care, and justice.

This book is an effort to offer some of those insights in a concise form. It is most definitely a joint effort. I've organized, shaped, and occasionally contributed some of the material, but it is usually in Keith's voice and from the fruit of his ministry with the staff of Good Works. The insights have been shaped by a community, not by Keith alone, as he would be the first to acknowledge. The sources for the material are varied. Some of it comes from the documents that the people at Good Works have generated over the years—especially the "Vision of Hope" statement, as well as from newsletters and occasional papers. Some comes from extensive interviews that I have done with Keith, and some from our more casual conversations, and some from interviews with several staff members. Hank Heschle was a student at Asbury Theological Seminary and an intern at Good Works. He also did a series of interviews with Keith, and some of the material comes from those conversations. Major themes and examples are derived from Keith's many presentations and the reflection papers he has written over the years.[7]

6. Like gardeners who set aside a special section of their gardens to monitor innovations in soil and fruitfulness of new plants, small communities can give evidence of the way Christian practices are lived out.

7. Several notable challenges in crafting this book emerged as I tried to preserve Keith's voice and yet combine all of the insights into a single presentation. How to effectively represent the wisdom of an entire community and credit the individual persons who articulated some of those insights raised other issues. As with many books that try to represent a

Three of Keith's favorite sayings capture his posture in the world: "Love is a verb," "Thank God I am not getting what I deserve," and "Love God. Love your neighbor. In the end, nothing else really matters." Darlene Wasserman, Keith's wife, who balances his intensity and fervor with her gentle and steady demeanor, is a major part of how his vision and passion took the form of shared meals and a welcoming community. While this is not a history of Good Works or a full description of their activities, many of the current activities and contexts are briefly described in the appendix. Additionally, the website (http://good-works.net) provides many resources, videos, photos, and stories.

Practices of discipleship and mission intersect and overlap in the pages of this book and in the lives of the Good Works community. Recognizing that we are often at risk for deceiving ourselves by being only hearers of the word and not doers, we emphasize how love for God and our neighbors is demonstrated in daily practices that express care, generosity, dignity, respect, and growth. Wisdom generated from lengthy experiences ministering with people who are poor, lonely, or without homes challenges some of our conventional notions of discipleship, community, service, and leadership. This book could be viewed as a collection of insights from a small band of folks living on the margins—some niche reflections. And to a certain extent, that would be true. But perhaps we should also be reminded of Jesus's own mission statement in Luke 4:18-19. At the start of his public ministry, he read from Isaiah and claimed it for his own calling:

---

dynamic, continually developing community, recognizing sources that have informally and orally shaped the community is difficult. We have chosen not to try to acknowledge individual contributions by name but are deeply indebted to the wisdom of many people.

Introduction

"The Spirit of the Lord is on me, because he has anointed
me to proclaim good news to the poor. He has sent me to
proclaim freedom for the prisoners and recovery of sight for
the blind, to set the oppressed free, to proclaim the year of
the Lord's favor."[8]

Good news to the poor, release for the oppressed, healing.
This is not a trendy niche. This is central—central for Jesus, and
central for his followers. Discipleship starts here, as we follow
the one who is good news for each of us.

Christine D. Pohl

---

8. Biblical quotations are taken from *Today's New International Version* unless otherwise noted.

ONE

Worship as Our Paradigm for Mission

Every day, we (staff and volunteers) bring our instruments and assemble for worship. Sometimes we bring well-tuned guitars and eager voices, but more often we are holding rakes, hammers, automotive repair equipment, counseling skills, a scrub brush, or a spatula. Whatever instruments we bring and whatever part we play, what we are doing is offered out of gratitude and adoration to God. Worship is our primary paradigm for mission.

But then, the Good Works community often takes this even further. We understand that part of our ministry is providing churches with opportunities to worship. Sometimes we describe our Work Retreat groups—the twenty-five to thirty-five short-term mission teams that come every year—as "worship teams." And the four hundred participants who build ramps, fix porches, or prepare meals are called "worshipers." They are sent out all over the county to the homes of widows or people dealing with the challenges of aging or disability. The instruments they bring and the work they do are as important as the songs we sing together. It's all worship if it is offered in a way that honors God and the people we hope to help.

CHAPTER ONE

Different Instruments but the Same Song

Think about how often you've heard or asked, "how was worship this week?" or said something like, "worship is really good at that church." What's the first image that comes to mind when you picture a worship team? We know what worship teams do, where they stand, and when they serve. But sometimes our definitions aren't big enough. Is it possible that the term *worship* has been taken hostage and locked up in a building where people gather for an hour or two on Sundays?

Worship usually involves prayer, singing, and Scripture reading. A worship service often includes some form of preaching or teaching, and perhaps liturgical elements like communion. A worship team helps lead in singing and praise. But does that exhaust the meaning of worship? Surely not for Paul, who writes in Romans 12:1: "Therefore, I urge you, brothers and sisters, in view of God's mercy, to offer your bodies as a living sacrifice, holy and pleasing to God—this is your true worship." What if worship involves much more than a song? What if it means a continual offering of ourselves to God and to others in acts of love, sacrifice, and thankfulness?

If we view the mission, ministry, and work God has trusted us with through the lens of worship, could we learn to see all that we do as an offering—a response—to God's mercy and goodness? Could it transform how we understand "going to church" or the way we divide Sunday morning worship from the rest of the week? How might it affect not just what we do but also how we do it?

Much has been written about worship, and this is just a small slice—but the connections among worship, care, justice, and mission are often overlooked. And yet, God has been concerned about these connections for thousands of years. In Amos 5:21, God tells Israel, "I hate, I despise your religious festivals"—

basically, I despise your worship. Can you imagine God saying that to us? Our beautiful worship—with our dynamic music programs and moving sermons? Could God really dislike *our* worship? How is that possible? In the times of Amos, Isaiah, and Micah, it was because of what else the people of God were and were not bringing to worship. It's not that there's necessarily something wrong with our prayers and praise songs, but those offerings are incomplete and become dangerous when we think they are sufficient for a faithful life (Matt. 23:23). A faithful life is meant to include much more—justice, holiness, and mercy. What could be wrong with our worship?

What could be wrong with our worship?

Jesus's words intensify these connections for his followers who want to be worshipers and who want to show their love for him. He identified himself with folks who needed care when he said, "'for I was hungry and you gave me something to eat, I was thirsty and you gave me something to drink, I was a stranger and you invited me in, I needed clothes and you clothed me, I was sick and you looked after me, I was in prison and you came to visit me,' . . . 'whatever you did for one of the least of these brothers and sisters of mine, you did for me'" (Matt. 25:35–36, 40). We often think it would be a privilege to serve Jesus as an act of worship, but Jesus himself says that in caring for the most vulnerable ones, we are serving him directly.

The implications for our worship and our lives are wonderful. Worship can take place in a house, church building, or at the home of a widow whose front porch is being rebuilt. Worship is not about location but about what is in our hearts. Because of this comprehensive understanding of worship in the Good Works community, we do not view ourselves as a social service agency, but instead, as a ministry whose primary mission is to love God and love people. Staff members seek to see everything we do as acts of worship. Everything. Acts of service and care are responses of gratitude for the love we have experienced. Part of our mission is providing the church with opportunities not just to "help" but also to worship.

In John 4:23, Jesus addresses expectations for the location of worship when he explains to the Samaritan woman that the Father seeks worshipers who worship in Spirit and truth. Perhaps if we understood that statement better, it would reshape how we view both worship and mission. God's longing for worshipers precedes even the call to go into all the world. We are called to seek the God who seeks us. What a beautiful mystery! Worship then is about truthfulness and integrity and the communion of our spirit with the Spirit of God, and it is God who equips worshipers to serve, persevere, and witness.

If worship is what we do as an offering of gratitude for the grace and goodness of God in our lives, it can take many different forms. One element of worship is simply adoration and praise of God. Another is love and service toward others. In an important way, we can stop trying to parse what is worship and what is not if we live our entire lives as living sacrifices, and if we view all of our work as somehow done unto the Lord. Done, offered, given as acts of love and worship.

Service as worship—and worship as service—both involve intentionality. Making a bed, doing the dishes, cleaning the bathroom are all expressions of worship when done with the attitude "this is for you, Lord." This broadened definition pushes us beyond our usual notions of worship to an entire way of viewing the world, ourselves, and ministry. A more comprehensive understanding of worship helps us pay attention to what stands behind and around everything we do. It's worship when we pray, "Lord, I want to be pleasing to you *in the way* I am doing this, not just in what I am doing."

Worship Transforms Our Service

We were created to worship. Either we will worship the Lord, or we will worship something or someone else, and seeing ourselves first as worshipers changes everything we usually think of as service. We recognize that, in God's gracious economy, our acts of love and care are good for us as well as for those we are helping. We cultivate teachable hearts and live as learners instead of seeing ourselves as experts at helping. And we realize that our acts of service should be carried out in ways that help us look like the One we are worshiping so that our efforts are marked by holiness, integrity, respect, yieldedness, and sacrifice.

Our task as worshipers is not to "fix" people but to love them. Whether we see change, whether we think we are having an impact, and whether someone is grateful or ungrateful for our help is less important—if it is all finally an offering of worship given as gratitude for the amazing grace and goodness of God. Of course, we want to see reconciled relationships; of course, we work hard to help people get jobs, find homes, experience hope, and make changes in their lives. Of course, we want to experience change in our lives, but when we see our efforts as responses of gratitude to God, it takes the pressure off and gives us freedom to take risks and move deeper into trust.

Worship involves sacrifice. Not animals or burnt offerings. Often it is the sacrifice of small things. Perhaps it is a sacrifice of time to be available to people, a sacrifice of individual preferences when I need to put my plans aside, a sacrifice of personal freedom so as not to cause harm to others or the ministry, a sacrifice of income to be fully present to neighbors in need. But that is also part of our call to offer ourselves as living sacrifices—"holy and pleasing to God" (Rom. 12:1).

Seeing all of our life as worship especially shapes how we evaluate our daily work. It means that our efforts are not primarily measured by success or by rules of efficiency. We don't reject success or avoid efficiency, but we subscribe to a different economy that places value on spending time with people, listening to them, giving ourselves to those who may not be able to repay us or provide a "good return on investment." This freedom to offer time generously in order to foster relationships distinguishes Good Works from many more traditional service agencies. We do not want people who come for assistance to feel as if they are interruptions or projects; it's important to stop what we are doing to engage someone who is visiting or needs our attention. Regardless of whether there is measurable success as a result of the time we've given, our effort has been an act of worship to the Lord.

For me (Keith), it was a journey toward seeing everything as worship. After becoming a follower of Jesus, I slowly realized that he wanted my entire life—what I did with my money, what kind of car I was going to drive, where I went on vacation, what I did in my "free time." I learned about submission to Christ and obedience. Out of this came the realization that God wanted me to submit my entire life, even who my friends were going to be. Later, I began to understand all of this as an act of worship.

First Things First: Loving God and Neighbor

Although worship takes different forms, loving God and loving our neighbors are always at the heart of it. The recipients of our love—God and neighbors—are connected, but loving God is our starting place, and the ordering of our loves should not be reversed. If we think that our task is to love our neighbors with all our heart, soul, mind, and strength and to love God as ourselves, we've wandered into bad theology—and troublesome psychological terrain.

Intentional times of emphasizing our vertical relationship with God are crucial; they are far more than nice extras in our busy days of ministry. They are central to keeping things in perspective, and they help to replenish our compassion and commitment. And they are important in their own right; because of God's immense love expressed to us through Jesus, we are awakened to respond back toward God with affection, trust, thanksgiving, and obedience.

Our worship also transforms how we see ourselves and others. It is the way we enter into the deeper places of our relationship with God where we can see ourselves as God sees us: valuable, broken, and made in his image—with dignity and purpose. In the same way, viewing the world through this bigger lens of worship of God helps us see our neighbors as God sees them, valuable, broken, and made in God's image—with dignity and purpose.[1] Being a worshiper provides a foundation for mutuality in relationships across differences in background and experience.

There is always a risk that understanding our care as worship or as ministry to Jesus displaces concern for the actual person in front of us. So we might take on an attitude that suggests, "I don't really care about you, this is for God." However, the person we are serving should never become less important because our motivation and accountability have been transformed and strengthened. Similarly, if we see our worship exclusively as care for others, we can overlook the importance of our first commitment to God.

When we serve people who are of special concern to God— widows, strangers, and fatherless children—we are offering

1. See, for example, Genesis 1:26-31; Psalm 8.

praise and adoration through our work.[2] It is "workship." Each day includes acts that require sacrifice. These acts (e.g., driving people places, cleaning, writing reports, gardening, etc.) often come with joy, but not always. Some are done simply because of our commitment to do what is right or needed. And doing the right thing is also an act of worship. To be able to say, "This is for you, Lord," when the work is hard and the persons we assist are less than fully appreciative, means we are able to continue to love in circumstances that are sometimes very difficult. This commitment sustains both the community and the individuals in it.

When we love people, we want what is best for them. We do not presume that we always know what that is, but we do know that love is far more than warm or friendly feelings. Love helps people grow in maturity, commitment, accountability, and a willingness to make sacrifices. Loving neighbors sometimes means providing a place for them to live, advocating for them, sharing a meal together, or sharing the good news of salvation in Christ. In other cases, it means giving persons a place of service so they too can love their neighbors.

Knowing Our Belovedness

Years ago, a mentor said to me (Keith): "Repeat after me: God loves me." Somehow, it sounded different and more personal than the familiar assurance that "God loves you." It spoke to me differently. To be loved by God, beloved of God, is an amazing gift that changes everything. My daily prayer is "Lord, help me to see people as you see them." Apart from God's telling me, I don't

2. See, for example, Exodus 22:21–22; Deuteronomy 14:28–29; 26:12–15; James 1:27.

know who I am or who they are. It's God's affirmation that we are his beloved. That's the launching pad for mission.

Am I loved? Do I have a purpose? People who don't believe they are loved or lovable are continually searching to fill their insecurity. Some turn to drugs, food, sex, or possessions to relieve or distract them, or try to find love in relationships that are destructive. People who know they are loved are more secure and less threatened by others who are concerned for them. They welcome accountability, are willing to take responsibility, are less likely to project their problems onto others, and can receive constructive criticism.

Questions about being loved and having purpose show up acutely in the lives of people who have lost their homes and support systems. But these are questions many of us struggle with—uncertainty about whether we are loved and have value apart from what we can do. In the context of worship, we learn and respond to how much God loves us. We learn that as God's *Am I loved? Do I have a purpose?* beloved, we can have hope about life, others, circumstances, and we can claim the assurance that nothing can separate us from that love (Rom. 8:38–39). On a day-to-day basis, most of us still struggle with uncertainty and confusion, so it is not all worked out in an instant. However, in an environment where people practice love for one another, we are regularly reassured of our belovedness and our value.

Even before Jesus began his ministry, he heard his Father say, "You are my Son, the Beloved; with you I am well pleased" (Mark 1:11 NRSV). God's affirmation of Jesus's identity provided the foundation of his ministry. Likewise, Jesus's new commandment to his disciples was to love one another just as he had loved them. We also begin our ministry by receiving the love of God. We can pray that we would hear God's voice say to each of us: "You are my beloved, with you I am well pleased."

We can manipulate people to say nice things about us, but true encouragement and reminders of belovedness are available from the body of Christ. God speaks both through others and through whispers of his Spirit regarding that belovedness. We can spur one another on toward goodness and wholeness out of a recognition of our belovedness. Knowing that we are loved affects both individuals and the character of the community itself. As one young woman who interned at Good Works for two summers explained, "I felt love—real, genuine and authentic love that propelled me to love others and accept myself in the process."

In the body of Christ, the formal and informal ways in which we talk to and about one another are powerful statements of how we perceive the other's value and belovedness, especially on the hard days. How we respond to unexpected visitors is an expression of how we see their belovedness and value. Not just the needy people who come, not only the person who is experiencing homelessness, but also the social worker trying to help her find a home. Each is affirmed and honored when we address them with care and respect and when we don't treat them as if they are an inconvenient interruption in our day.

Knowing our belovedness frees us to give our lives as an offering

Recognition of a person's belovedness and value are also offered when we take time in staff or community meetings to give attention to someone who is upset or in crisis. While the agenda for a meeting cannot be disrupted every time someone has a particular problem, we can be careful that our responses contribute to folks feeling cared for and valued.

The decision to emphasize each person's belovedness, and being willing to linger on this, is also an economic decision. It is costly in terms of time and resources. But every community makes choices about how it invests its resources, and choosing to be worship-oriented rather than results-oriented means that sacrifice, love, and affirmation are complexly intertwined. Knowing our belovedness frees us to give our lives as an offering with the confidence that what we give is of value to God. Even when we don't see results quickly, we can have peace and confidence that our sacrificial expressions of worship are precious to God.

Gratitude: Vertical Thanksgiving/Horizontal Affirmation

Gratitude prompts and shapes our responses to God, often expressed in times of worship and thanksgiving. But gratitude can also shape our communal life and service.[3] When we function well as the body of Christ, we are honoring Jesus and demonstrating our gratitude for his grace in our lives. We spur one another on toward wholeness and holiness; we help each other to identify and celebrate our natural and spiritual gifts. When we give each person a place in the community, we also honor Jesus.

A posture of gratitude challenges us to make time for affirmation in community. One role of leadership in the body of Christ is to facilitate affirmation as a form of gratitude. Affirmation can be offered in structured times that include verbal recognition in community, in private written cards, texts, or emails, and in annual celebration events.

A staff member described her experience at Good Works:

We have developed intentional practices of affirmation and gratitude. . . . In our meetings, someone sitting across the room from you might be saying positive things they notice about you. It's obvious they're not just making these things

3. See, for example, Psalms 30:11-12; 105:1-6; 136.

up to be encouraging. They really have watched and noticed these things in you. And their words are offered to God and to you as a gift. Good Works doesn't usually connect the dots and say, "Well I just want you to know we've had worship now," but it's obvious that something really good is happening in the community, something life-giving is going on.

A challenging issue in ministry and service is giving up our need to be thanked by the people we serve, but it is made easier when we are located in a culture of gratitude and affirmation. When people are neither grateful nor responsive to our help, it is important to "lay down" our need to be thanked. In these instances, we must turn to Jesus and the community and learn to find satisfaction in these acts as "offerings." Otherwise, we may be tempted to respond with resentment, anger, or even manipulation so that we feel appreciated. It hurts, but this daily dying is part of the fabric of worship. When we care for people, but they reject our love and concern, we respond by grieving together as a community and by offering one another encouragement.

In Good Works' staff meetings, the affirmations from donors and thank you notes from recipients are read aloud as a regular way of providing encouragement. While we must be careful to avoid the presumption that can come with praise and recognition, such encouragements do help in creating a culture that is resilient and joy filled.

Kingdom of God Paradigm

As noted in the introduction, Good Works exists to "connect people from all walks of life with people in poverty so that the Kingdom of God can be experienced." This is the mission statement of the community. But what does poverty have to do with

God's kingdom? And why would anyone think that deliberately making those connections among people would lead to "experiencing" the kingdom of God?

Is it really possible to "experience" the kingdom or reign of God today? The Gospels give us clues regarding what it might look like. The reign of God is where God's power is active: the blind receive their sight, the lame walk, those with leprosy are cleansed, the deaf hear, the dead are raised, those who are poor have good news brought to them (Luke 7:20-23). When a community is surrendered to the movement of God's healing Spirit, God's miraculous work of redemption and release continues. Sometimes the work is slow and quiet, and sometimes it goes unnoticed by individuals and the community, but it does move forward to bring healing and wholeness.

The good news of the kingdom will always involve healing of some kind

The good news of the kingdom will always involve healing of some kind. It is where the cycle of violence loses its grip and a circle of forgiveness begins. It is where people, communities, and creation flourish under God's reign of love.

Jesus explained that he came to call not the righteous but sinners (Matt. 9:13), and, for us to experience the kingdom, we need to recognize our own sinful attitudes and actions. The kingdom of God is where we continually repent from our sins, receive God's mercy and grace to take responsibility for those sins, and live as servants of the Lord of mercy by extending mercy and steadfast love to others. This kingdom living is the posture of worship.

In Luke 1:46-55, the reign of God is described as where the people who are lowly and poor are blessed, shown mercy, lifted up, filled with good things, and remembered. Throughout the Scriptures, we see widows, orphans, and strangers given a special place in God's care, and those who are poor are singled out for God's concern and value. We experience the kingdom of God when a community embodies these concerns and welcomes outsiders and vulnerable persons. We experience the kingdom when a community continues to renounce injustice for the sake of economic gain, excessive wealth, and pride and when that community chooses instead to share its resources with those in need and trusts God to sustain all of us (Matt. 6:25-34).

The kingdom of God is now and among us today, but it is also "not yet." Our glimpses of the kingdom here on earth are signs that point us toward the kingdom in its eternal fullness. As a result, our kingdom experiences often appear small and insignificant, like little mustard seeds. Small as they are, mustard seeds sprout and grow like crazy (Mark 4:30-32)! In Matthew 6:33, Jesus calls us to seek first his kingdom and his righteousness. With that as our first priority, our mission is amazingly comprehensive and profoundly important.

Discipleship: Connecting Worship and Justice

Becoming followers of Jesus means that the mission of Jesus becomes our mission; the people he noticed and loved become the people we notice and love. The words Jesus used to announce his ministry on earth have a strong claim on us as his followers: "The Spirit of the Lord is on me, because he has anointed me to proclaim good news to the poor. He has sent me to proclaim freedom for the prisoners and recovery of sight for the blind, to set the oppressed free, to proclaim the year of the Lord's favor" (Luke 4:18-19).

This is also our calling. Jesus has given us his Spirit; *the Spirit of the Lord is on us*. We too are anointed to bring good news to the poor, healing to the broken, and release to those in bondage.

Obeying this calling from God requires us to wrestle with what it means for our context, our time, our place. Three questions arise immediately: First, what is the good news? Second, who are the poor? And third, how do we share the gospel with them? Searching for answers to these questions lies at the heart of our discipleship. They are questions for every Christian community.

If we are anointed to bring good news to the poor, what does that mean? Perhaps we can understand it as God giving the followers of Jesus a special dispensation of grace to persevere in loving people who have been hurt, violated, or excluded and are unresponsive. Because of the harm they've experienced, some have turned to unhealthy and unholy patterns of living, and some have become difficult to help. When combined with difficult external circumstances and injustice, their situations can be challenging, to say the least. And life-changing assistance is impossible apart from God's grace.

Becoming followers of Jesus means that the mission of Jesus becomes our mission

The ministry with which God has entrusted most of us is not primarily about buildings, programs, techniques, or methods. Rather, God has trusted us with people—neighbors—to serve and love. In Matthew 25:14-30, we read a story of a master who entrusted his property and resources to three servants. When the master returned, he rewarded or punished his servants based on how they had managed his money—how they had stewarded his resources. Immediately following this passage is the familiar description of how the nations will be judged. Those who will inherit the kingdom are those who responded to the needs of people who were hungry and thirsty, welcomed the stranger, clothed the naked, and visited the sick and the prisoner. We also will be asked to account for our stewardship toward our neighbors—especially those who are poor.

Jesus's life on earth gives us a picture of what it means to do this. As he went through the cities and villages, he proclaimed the good news of the kingdom, and cured disease and sickness. He embodied the coming of the kingdom by being friends with people who were poor and by sharing meals with them. In doing so, he brought hope in the form of physical healing, and freedom from spiritual, emotional, and social bondage. Bestowing on them God's forgiveness, Jesus released people from the cycle of sin's consequences. But Jesus's mission was bigger than his individual work; he said to his disciples, "The harvest is plentiful but the workers are few. Ask the Lord of the harvest, therefore, to send out workers into his harvest field" (Matt. 9:37–38).

Before ascending to heaven, Jesus gave his disciples further directions about how to continue the work he had inaugurated while on earth. He commissioned them, saying: "All authority in heaven and on earth has been given to me. Therefore go and make disciples of all nations, baptizing them in the name of the Father and of the Son and of the Holy Spirit, and teaching them to obey everything I have commanded you. And surely I am with you always, to the very end of the age" (Matt. 28:18–20).

As followers of Jesus, we too are given this calling to make disciples and encourage them in obedience to Christ. Our worship of God overflows into a lifestyle of bold expression of the faith that motivates us. This communication of the good news happens through both *demonstration* and *proclamation*, as we embody lifestyles of love and tell and teach others about the love of Christ. Much of our witness is simply *overflow*. As Jesus has touched our lives, we are changed and more able to share that love with others.

Each of us, then, is called to be a disciple and to make disciples. Serving those who are struggling with poverty is an important way by which God develops people into mature disciples.

As much as those struggling with poverty might need assistance, disciples of Christ with more material resources need to serve. In the Good Works community, half of our ministry involves loving God and people in need, and thus fulfilling the Great Commandment. The other half involves inviting others into this life of discipleship, which fulfills the Great Commission. To do this, Good Works structures a variety of safe yet challenging opportunities for people from all walks of life to engage with and serve those in need. Some avenues are designed for those who want to commit to an entry-level experience. *At Good Works, everyone can expect to be changed* Other contexts provide opportunities for a deeper commitment. But maturing in discipleship and grace also means that those with power and resources learn to approach relationships with people in need with deep humility. Each has something valuable to offer the other.

The practices of discipleship available through the traditional structures of the church are not always expansive enough to challenge believers to mature in faith by asking them to interact with folks different from themselves. At Good Works, everyone can expect to be changed—by the various environments that are catalysts for people to grow up in Christ. People frequently comment, "Your ministry is to people in poverty or homelessness." Yes, but no, that's not the entirety of it. The mission of Good Works is not only to bring hope to people experiencing economic poverty. Instead, we desire for God to use us to impart wholeness into the life of each person we come to know. All of us, rich or poor or somewhere in between, are in need of God's healing in the most basic relationships of life—with ourselves, other people, God, and creation. In our relationships with people who are not Christians but want to help others, we hope to create opportunities for them not only to do good but also to explore questions about life and God.

Demonstrating and proclaiming the gospel can occur in many different ways. Some folks will come to experience the love of Christ through serving people in poverty. Others will experience God's grace by receiving care and assistance. For some, we can plant the first seed of faith into a person's life, and other times, our role is to nurture a growing faith in Christ. Sometimes we simply prepare people to be receptive to Jesus. Like a plow, we can get the rocks out of the soil of the heart so that good things can be planted there later.

At Good Works, other avenues for being witnesses of Jesus are also available. These include opportunities to share with staff members of local agencies who are working with the same people as are being served by Good Works. Because all truth is God's truth, it is a privilege to be taught both by our Christian and non-Christian friends in the helping professions. To the degree that those in the helping professions help people know the truth, we can join hands with them and work together. The trust that we build with local agencies and authorities benefits all of us, and it certainly helps the people being served.

Intimacy with Christ: The Personal Side of Worship

Nurturing intimacy with Christ doesn't simply mean that "Jesus and I are feeling good about each other." Knowing Jesus involves love and knowledge that transforms every aspect of our lives—sensing a fresh urgency to spend time with him, especially if we spend much of the day doing challenging work. We know Christ in the Scriptures, in prayer and conversation, in silence and listening, and in lament and heartache.

Can we be in conversation with Jesus as we repair a porch or advise a teen runaway? Of course. Is Christ present with us when we walk through the woods on a gorgeous day or spend time in a retreat setting? Of course. When we attend to a cranky toddler or a confused senior? Of course. Do we have to work at this underlying, ongoing conversation? Yes. Do we also need times when our focus is less divided, when the conversation is more intimate? Always.

As we learn to trust more fully in Jesus, we are better able to identify our own brokenness, experience real forgiveness, and earnestly try to change the way we live in order to please him. Jesus transforms our shame—especially as he works through our communities—and allows us to forgive ourselves and those who have sinned against us. The Spirit of God fills us, adding to our faith and bringing power to transform our lives. From the overflow of gratitude for what we have received and experienced, we can invite others into a life with Jesus.

Embracing the necessity of having a daily time set aside with God is a nonnegotiable for Good Works staff members. It is expressed in a regular message that I (Keith) bring to the staff about "being on," which has everything to do with making sure that, when you begin your assignment that day, you've done your preparation. You're not just showing up. You have taken time to make sure you're not carrying something—unconfessed—into relationships or activities or responsibilities of the day. We emphasize individual time in Scripture and in prayer as a prerequisite to fruitfulness in ministry. Do we demand accountability in that? No—but we expect it. And it's obvious when people are not prepared.

The structures and leadership of a community can formalize some practices and expectations, but there must also be spontaneous events that move people into a deeper walk with Christ.

There is a communal aspect of nurturing individual intimacy with Christ. Some of that is formed when folks go out and do things together and afterward realize that the shared tasks have bonded them in ways that reinforce their prayers and reading of Scripture. Sometimes a deeper walk comes as we minister together to someone or navigate a crisis with him or her.

At our Friday night gatherings, people frequently ask me, "Keith, will you pray for me?" And I say, "Absolutely. Let me go find Chris," and he'll join us. Part of that is ministering as a team. On any given Friday night, there are probably six people I can pick from the staff, and others who are not on the staff but who I know love the Lord and are part of the community, and I'll pull them in as well. I'm trying to model this for the community—I don't want to be the only person folks come to for prayer.

It's easy to become so absorbed in the work of ministry and community, discipleship and care, that we become blind to how little we are attending directly to our relationship with Christ. Then suddenly we become aware of how empty, vulnerable, or weary we are, how involved we are in Christian ministry but simultaneously how far from God we feel. We can help each other with this and cultivate a culture that recognizes the importance of rhythms of solitude and ministry, sabbath and engagement. Years after we began our work, our community built a retreat cabin for solitary retreats to nurture the internal life of workers. And while someone spends time on retreat, the community keeps that person in prayer.

Conclusion

As our paradigm for mission, worship shapes and infuses our individual and community life, our character, and our practices.

The God we worship desires upright hearts—integrity—in our thoughts and behavior. Worship helps us see correctly—it influences our perspective and our leadership practices. It infuses our good works with a different spirit. Worship stands behind and operates within all of the following chapters.

Prayer

Lord, give us a holy desperation for your presence in our lives so that we can say with Moses, if your presences does not go with us, do not send us from this place (Exod. 33:15). We are dependent on you—on your love, power, grace, and wisdom. Free us from misplaced confidence in methods, buildings, and money. Cultivate in us hearts full of gratitude. Help us to live into our belovedness and give us grace to respond to others with the love you have shown us.
Amen.

Questions for Reflection and Discussion

1.   What elements, activities, and attitudes do you associate with worship?
2.   In what ways do sacrifice and joy shape your experience of worship?
3.   When you have found it hard to love someone, how has it helped you to see expressions of love to that person as a way of loving and serving God?
4.   In what ways do you sense or know that you are God's "beloved child"? How has that affected the way you value your life and the lives of others?
5.   In your ministry context, how are persons reminded that

they are beloved children of God, that intimacy with God is crucial to ministry, and that the community wants every person to flourish?

6. How might a more intentional emphasis on gratitude and affirmation strengthen your community?

7. In what settings do you see worship, care, and justice connected?

8. How does individual closeness to Christ strengthen and shape your witness and work?

TWO

Integrity Matters

A number of years ago, at a meeting of Christian organizations engaged in caring for people without homes, Good Works staff members were uncertain about how to respond to the conference's emphasis on programs and programming. Did what we were doing with people who were experiencing homelessness represent "programs" we could talk about? Good Works thinks in terms of building relationships more than developing programs, and as one staff member explained, "our program is integrity." It is about relationships and building higher and higher levels of trust, always asking whether a particular behavior or response is going to build or diminish trust. So, as we have frequently reminded one another since that conference, "if we don't have integrity, we don't have a program."

If we don't have integrity, we don't have a program

Why should the emphasis placed on integrity by one small organization matter for the church? Actually, there are plenty of reasons. Fruitful ministry, especially with those who have been abused, betrayed, or hurt, depends on trust; and trust depends on integrity. In addition, countless ministries and churches have faltered on the shoals of dishonesty, deception, and self-serving aggrandizement—all failures in integrity. We, as disciples of Jesus, need to think long and hard about integrity and about how it is expressed in our individual and corporate lives.

Even when organizations intend to help persons in need, they sometimes provide assistance in a way that "fills their hands but breaks their hearts" by overlooking the importance of integrity and respect in relationships.[1] Other organizations, so intent on helping folks, neglect the well-being of their own staff members and volunteers and eventually find themselves dealing with staff and helpers who leave hurt, burned out, cynical, angry, or feeling misused.

Integrity matters; it matters a lot. In a time when our focus, even in the church, is so often on results or on "getting it done," integrity can seem like an inconvenient moral demand that can be ignored "just this once" for the sake of a more important goal. Often, our goals are good, but we forget that *how* we accomplish them matters as much as *that* we accomplish them. On a day-to-day basis, especially when dealing with vulnerable people, integrity is closely connected to how we use power and to viewing others with respect. It is the bedrock of building trust.

Integrity is made up of truthfulness and fidelity; it requires wisdom and discernment. It is connected to faithfulness, purity, reliability, and honesty. From the Scriptures, we understand that God promotes people to responsibility according to their faithfulness in little and their faithfulness in much.[2] One of the verses that has continued to shape my (Keith's) life is: "He considered me faithful, putting me into service" (1 Tim. 1:12 NASB).

At Good Works, integrity is central. Recognizing the daily challenges and occasional failures, a staff member explains, "It's

1. Philip Hallie, *Tales of Good and Evil, Help and Harm* (New York: Harper Collins, 1997), 207.
2. See, for example, Matthew 25:14–30.

not because we get it right every time, but because we recognize its importance and care deeply about it. We have made it central to our life together, to ministry and to our individual lives. Our insights aren't necessarily new or original, but they have been embodied in a community over time."

When our lives and desires are open and oriented to pleasing God, there is little room for hiding in the dark corners of half-heartedness, hypocrisy, or deceit. The way we act and speak, and the people and things we value, should be consistent because what we do emerges from who we are. Our thoughts, feelings, words, and actions flow from our identity as God's children who desire to offer praise with an upright heart (Ps. 119:7). Our ministry, then, is only as strong as each member's integrity and the integrity of the community's decisions and practices. A simple, working definition that the Good Works community uses for integrity is "what you do when you think no one is looking and no one will ever find out."

What we do emerges from who we are

Living Truthfully

A culture of truthfulness can be fostered in many ways. For example, when the Good Works staff, volunteers, and friends gather for prayer, song, sharing, and teaching each week, there is also a time set aside to "linger" in silence. A combination of song and silence presses on each of us to be conscious of where we stand with others relationally. Sometimes we explore the meaning of a particular worship song and ask questions to provoke a deeper, more truth-filled worship: *What does this song say about who we are in Christ, and what does this song say about who Christ is in us?* Because so much of our community's theology is formed through worship, it is an opportunity to reflect on the core values of living in reconciled, truthful relationships and building unity.

Truthfulness is central to integrity. In Psalm 51:6, David reminds us that God desires "truth in the innermost being" (NASB). Truthfulness is more than saying hard things to one another. It is a way of life and a way of offering our worship that involves being careful that our words and intentions align, and that we speak words that are accurate to the facts but also build people up.[3]

If, in ministry, we do not live out truthfulness and reconciliation with one another every day, we will be powerless to implore others to be in a right relationship with God. In addition, truthful relationships and right worship are deeply connected, and the connection should be intentionally reinforced on a regular basis.

Some well-intentioned Christians struggle with understandings of holiness or sanctification that result in people hiding their sin or denying their pain. But only honesty about our sin among trusted friends or coworkers, and truthfulness about our need for healing, will allow Christians to reach out and receive help from others with whom they are ministering. This is crucial in intra-staff relationships and in healthy communities.

A willingness to have Christ work in us is manifested as we give and receive permission to speak truthfully into each other's lives. When the community is functioning as the body of Christ, it is one of the ways that God grows us into maturity. It isn't always easy or pleasant, and it certainly doesn't fit the cultural emphasis on always feeling good about ourselves. Truth can

3. For a fuller discussion of living truthfully in community, see Christine D. Pohl, *Living into Community: Cultivating Practices That Sustain Us* (Grand Rapids: Eerdmans, 2012), chapters 8–10.

be challenging, and biblical standards are high. It is important to realize that we have to stretch ourselves to love one another and to love the truth. We can help each other to love in the hard places, and that often involves sacrifice, inconvenience, and difficulty. Combining a tough and tender love requires a community that cares deeply for one another.

Truthfulness can be quickly undermined by an anti-community practice of gossip. For example, prayer requests that divulge unnecessary information about someone to others not involved in the concern can make a community unsafe and unkind. Community is protected when we speak about one another with honor and respect, and when we maintain appropriate boundaries in talking about each other. Ephesians 4 reminds us to put off falsehood and speak truthfully to one another because we are members of one body, and only to speak what is helpful for building others up. One way this is done at Good Works is by maintaining a commitment to speaking only positive words about a fellow staff member when he or she is absent from the gathering.

In a tight-knit community that is continually ministering with folks who are deeply wounded and vulnerable, it is important to be very attentive to staff behavior. An incident at Good Works illustrates this: Over a period of weeks during staff meetings, some real tension between two staff members was evident in their attitudes (e.g., rolling eyes) and in the tone that they used with each other. Probing further, it was clear that beneath Jenna's outward demeanor, there was hurt, frustration, and a growing sense of resentment.[4] Because of our years of experience together in the Good Works community, I (Keith) knew it was clear to her what her responsibility was and that she only needed some encouragement and support to go to Jack and speak

4. Names have been changed.

with him. We emphasize that each one of us must take responsibility for the initiative of "going." It was my role simply to remind Jenna of what she already knew she had to do. Soon afterward, Jenna approached Jack and they had a long talk that proved to be a catalyst to addressing other issues. In this case, Jack was not aware of the particular behaviors that were causing Jenna to be so offended, and the matter was brought to a good resolution—a resolution that continues to this day. My own follow-up with the situation seemed rather minimal, because the two parties handled the matter so well.

The personal maturity of both Jenna and Jack played a significant role in the resolution of the conflict, but the spiritual infrastructure of the community was also important. Community expectations, modeling, and truth-telling practices were the invisible background that enabled this situation and many like it to remain limited in impact. Of course, occasionally tensions are more difficult to resolve and reveal some of the challenges we each face in dealing with different interpersonal styles, individual woundedness, sin, and immaturity.

At the start of employment at Good Works, every staff contract includes the expectation that the new staff person will write a short essay on "conflict transformation." In an effort to help people learn to assume that conflict is normal and resistance to it is problematic, it asks each staff person to reflect on how he or she plans to resolve conflicts. It is a proactive way of building community.

Recognizing that difficulties in staff relationships and persistent sin of individual members can harm the entire community and its ministry means that those concerns must be addressed even when it is difficult, awkward, or time-consuming to do so. It is helpful to see this too as an act of worship offered up to the Lord. The importance of this practice is reinforced by the very disturbing story from the Old Testament in Joshua 7:1–26, where the sin of one man—Achan—in the Israelite community brings great harm to the larger community and total destruction to Achan and his family.[5] We are warned also in Hebrews 12:15 of our responsibility to be sure that "no bitter root grows up to cause trouble and defile many." In our quite individualistic culture, we like to imagine that individual choices affect only ourselves. In communities, however, what seem like individual sins (e.g., bitterness or resentment) can impact and spread through the entire community.

Another way to sustain a culture of truthfulness in community is to encourage each member to "keep it in the light." Recognizing Jesus's warning that what has been "said in the dark will be heard in the daylight" (Luke 12:3), we can embrace the gift of community that keeps us from hiding inappropriate or destructive behaviors and relationships.[6] Community matures and thrives when persons do this on their own initiative, rather than waiting until leaders recognize and address such issues.

Cultivating Trust and Respect

When a ministry is based on relationships, its currency is trust and respect. It is remarkably easy to undermine both by careless actions or thoughtless words. Questions or demands that unnecessarily intrude into people's lives, story-telling that makes

5. Despite explicit commands not to touch the spoils of war, Achan secretly took some of the "devoted things" or spoils and hid them in his tent.

6. This emphasis on "keeping it in the light" also has a more specific application among the staff and volunteers of Good Works and will be discussed further in chapter 4.

people into objects, and funding requirements that ask for more information about recipients than is needed undermine respect and trust.

A Christian ministry is continually challenged to make choices that demonstrate respect and trust. Good Works has turned down grants that required reporting more information about recipients than was warranted and has chosen to not tell many stories about the residents because of the risk of misusing them. Even the language and vocabulary used in describing residents communicate a particular view and valuing of persons.

In ministries that depend heavily on volunteers to work alongside staff members, the maturity and wisdom of the volunteers often varies and can affect those who have come to receive help. Practices that involve communicating our faith are complex when working with vulnerable persons who need the material assistance that the community can provide. In Good Works' case, this has led to very clearly articulated expectations for staff and volunteers—expectations that are regularly discussed:

1. **Earn the right to speak.** Don't assume your title or credentials give you that right. Don't assume that because a person is in need and you are working there or you're a volunteer that you have such rights. It is important to work to establish trust and earn the right to share your story or a verbal presentation of the gospel.

2. **Use respect as the primary lens through which you conduct the relationship.** If people don't feel respected, you undermine your message. Every person has dignity and deserves honor; that means giving attention to your tone, timing, and how you say what you say.

3. **Assume that God has been at work long before you came on the scene.** This person didn't just show up; God's been working with him or her. In humility, ask the Lord,

"how can I further your work of love and grace in this person's life?" Recognize that whatever you have to say about your faith and your relationship with God is offered in the context of what already exists inside each person you meet.

4. **Get permission.** There isn't any reason why you can't simply ask, "Bill, would it be OK if I told you a little of my story for 2-3 minutes?" If he says "no," that's fine. Respect that. His act of saying "no" is part of his contending with God. But if he says "yes," then start with your own story. And that story is where you intersect with his story as the first point of connection.

Especially if persons come into a community primarily because of a need in their lives for things like food or shelter, it is appropriate to *ask* them whether we can share the story of Christ's love with them. Getting permission might also come in the form of *asking* whether we can pray for them. Because Good Works is a Christian ministry and desires that every person comes to know Christ, there are tensions. But because we recognize the constant risks of coercion and dishonesty, commitments to respect and care are taken very seriously.

It is important to try to hold together respect for a person's request to be left alone and our eagerness to find ways to engage them in conversation and relationship. We need wisdom to discern when we are respecting their choices and when it is our fear of being rejected that keeps us from sharing the good news of God's love. Christian communities often struggle with cultivating a tender, sensitive, holy boldness about the gospel.

When people in our volunteer community are especially zealous about sharing their faith, they must nevertheless submit to these guidelines to continue to serve with Good Works. Those who have been unwilling to agree to the expectations are often good Christian folks, but on rare occasions, the leadership of Good Works has had to say, "You know, I don't think there's a good fit here." Some volunteers don't acknowledge or consider the fact that when a person's food, shelter, or help depends on our response to them, we have enormous power in their lives.

As a community, we have learned to be very attentive to power in relationships, and to be careful not to manipulate people into hearing about Jesus or into saying they are Christians simply because they need practical assistance. Good Works does not hold required worship meetings or Bible studies as a condition of people receiving help. However, residents are invited to join the community in our worship times, and the good news is shared in ways that reflect trust in God's ongoing work.

Truthful, trusting relationships among staff members and volunteers provide a healthy check on how power is used in the lives of vulnerable people. At Good Works, every staff person, intern, and volunteer is asked to make a commitment to use their power for good—for what is in the best interest of those being served and of the community at large. When our use of power is not anchored in the fear of God and in commitments to one another, we are more likely to become abusers and oppressors ourselves.

Cultivating trust and respect applies also to how staff and volunteers are treated by each other, by the leadership, and by those who seek assistance. The operating commitments for Good Works include some tensions: a commitment to serving others regardless of whether they are grateful—but also a recognition that under no circumstances should staff or volunteers be expected to take any form of abuse from those being served. The community also recognizes that all service requires some measure of sacrifice, and staff and volunteers should expect to be challenged emotionally, psychologically, and spiritually. In all cases, the personal growth of staff and volunteers is as important as the personal growth of the people being served.

This commitment to the well-being of staff and volunteers is crucial in the life of Good Works. Volunteers are not "used" for ministry. When volunteers, donors, recipients, and staff are all viewed as part of ministry, it fits the mission of "connecting people from all walks of life with people in poverty so the Kingdom of God can be experienced." This is the mutuality of ministry, such that the people who volunteer become as important a focus as those who receive assistance.

Accountability

Accountability operates in different ways. With top-down accountability, people in our lives hold us accountable because we've invited them to do so, or because it is somehow their responsibility (e.g., bosses, supervisors). In some cases, we might ask individuals to help us "walk in the light" and give them permission to speak truthfully into our lives. We can work out questions for them to ask us that will keep us moving toward growth and wholeness. Another form is bottom-up accountability, which involves a recognition that how we live is a witness to the people around us, and they notice how we behave. We cultivate holy habits in part because we know others are watching and asking questions, and because we don't want to cause others to stumble. There is also peer-to-peer accountability involving friends whom we cannot impress. We need encouragement, but we also need friends who will tell us the truth about ourselves. For married people, there is another level of accountability in the spousal relationship. Spouses know our patterns, and when they ask, "What's wrong?" or "What's going on?" they usually know our foibles and points of weakness.

Having people in our lives whom we cannot impress is crucial for shaping the character and practices of faithful disciples of Jesus and especially crucial for any good leader. The higher up we move in terms of status, recognition, or power, the lonelier and more insulated we can often become. Frequently, there is also less accountability. Having people and structures in place to help leaders recognize danger spots and self-deception is essential. When no one challenges them, those with the most power are in the most danger and are the most dangerous.

One former staff member shared a memory from the early days of Good Works that has shaped his own posture in ministry for many years. He recounts:

> Tension and frustration were building between Keith and another staff member, and Keith exploded in a meeting—becoming super angry with him. It was totally inappropriate and incommensurate to the problem. I hit the breaking point over how Keith had been treating this staff member and also snapped in the meeting in front of everyone else. I stopped the meeting, declaring how wrong Keith's behavior had been. People rarely challenged or corrected Keith like that, and my approach was not exemplary. But later in the day, Keith and I talked at length, and he was responsive and grateful, recognizing his failure and apologizing to the person with whom he had been so angry. Keith was ready to make amends. One result of this messy event was that Keith's and my relationship deepened. He had failed, but his response to a coworker calling him out deepened trust. Later, I was chosen to be acting director of Good Works for a year while Keith was traveling. Now an executive director of another organization myself, my experience at Good Works regarding the importance of a leader's accountability has stayed with me.

An important part of accountability involves reflecting on our use of power in community. Often Christians are uncomfortable with the notion that we have power, but if our power is not recognized, especially in working with vulnerable people, it can be very destructive. Overt uses of power can be oppressive, but more covert forms such as manipulation can also be dangerous and tempting.

An important part of accountability involves reflecting on our use of power in community

A force that often undermines integrity and diminishes our effectiveness in ministry is our personal woundedness kept hidden because of fear. Establishing accountability partners helps bring those wounds and hurts into the light where the impact of that woundedness on others is clear and where we can find healing. Giving people leadership responsibilities when they are unable or unwilling to deal with their own wounds is often a recipe for disaster.

Good Works combines a high level of personal freedom, initiative, and agency with a high level of accountability. Imagine ownership, accountability, and autonomy as the three points of a triangle. The lines between the points are not the same length for everyone, but everyone is operating in each area. A staff member describes how this is worked out in community: "We resist intruding into areas that are not our responsibility, and we practice respect while expecting and cultivating individual responsibility. Each volunteer is connected to a specific staff person, and interns experience a rigorous discernment process."

Sometimes a commitment to accountability requires sacrificing positive recognition and possible monetary support. When a major television network wanted to do a feature story on Good Works, the staff asked that the reporter agree to visit with the community long enough to understand its practices and commitments (a several-day visit). When the network wouldn't consent to that level of accountability, Good Works forfeited the possibility of national recognition, wary that the reporting might turn their residents into objects for the evening news.

Practicing "Clear"

To sustain a community that values integrity and lives truthfully, it is important to have simple structures in place. Such structures can create expectations in the community that certain attitudes and behaviors are unacceptable. For example, while patience and forgiveness are central to Christian identity, and while a willingness to overlook offenses is commended in Proverbs 19:11, allowing bitterness to take hold in response to "overlooked" offenses is disastrous (Heb. 12:15). Confronting interpersonal difficulties and addressing issues truthfully are crucial for forgiveness and reconciliation.

Christ's forgiveness of our sins and then empowering us to forgive others is what makes the good news good. Forgiveness is the centerpiece of the gospel and an important litmus test of maturity—particularly because Jesus puts it at the center of his prayer, "forgive us our sins as we forgive," and because Jesus gives us the power to do it.

Over the years, Good Works has cultivated a practice called "Clear" and has built it into our weekly community gatherings. This practice recognizes that if we're going to work together, we're going to step on one another's toes. We're going to say things that we'll need to apologize for. And on the other side, we're going to have to deal with addressing someone who said or did something that offended or hurt us (Matt. 5:24). This is the normal atmosphere of Christian community. Knowing that, it is important to build some structure in our life together to deal with challenges that come up—preferably at least once a week.

At Good Works, this is handled a little differently by different staff members. Each has a unique way of asking the same questions. But in the leadership meetings, one way or another, the facilitator asks, "Are we 'Clear'?" which means, "How are we doing?" And most days, it's "Clear," "Clear," "Clear." It feels a little formal, but it's really important, because if each person is not "Clear" and we go on with the business of the day—making decisions about money or people or programs—it's contaminated by the fact that we haven't worked through some things among ourselves. Sometimes, a person will say, "I need to talk about something." And that could take ten minutes, or it could take our entire time together, which displaces our regular business! We might wonder, "What do we do now? We didn't get to anything." But actually, we got to what was most important—the value of reconciled relationships. And if we can't work on reconciled relationships with each other, we are powerless to tell people to be reconciled to God.

Forgiveness is the centerpiece of the gospel and an important litmus test of maturity

So "Clear" becomes a regular opportunity to make sure no one is carrying anything against another person. It means holding together two commitments: first, knowing that love covers a multitude of sins, and therefore not saying anything and just forgiving the other person; and second, remembering Jesus's words that if your brother or sister sins, go and tell him or her (Matt. 18:15). How do you know which is the right response? Many of us have been socially trained not to say anything. Meanwhile we're stewing, bothered, and disturbed. How do we help people sort out these tensions?

At Good Works, generally we have found that if we start with overlooking and forgiving, but are honest enough with ourselves to say, "This isn't working, and I need to talk about it," it can be sorted out. Because if you're not able to let go of the problem—and that's not the same for everybody—then you do need to talk and pray about it. And you need to know from each of us that if one of us has sinned against you, that person wants to be humble enough to ask your forgiveness and wants to work on the problem.

Here's an example of how this has worked at Good Works: One of my coworkers said to me, "Keith, when you sing, you sing really loud, and it bothers me. Could you just go to the other side of the room, because I don't want you to sing next to me." Well, first of all, I thanked her, because I want to hear this; and second of all, now that I'm aware of it, we laugh about it, and I check in with her and ask, "How am I doing with the singing thing?" As soon as I knew my behavior was disturbing her, it became my responsibility to be a little sensitive to her about it. But it doesn't remove her responsibility to also put up with me: I think she knows I'm not trying to harm her; and I'm not doing it to irritate her. So there's a tension here, and I think all these things come up as we try to work out the experience of our salvation with "fear and trembling." In Philippians 2, Paul reminds the church to "have the same attitude of mind Christ Jesus had," and in humility to put others first, "being one in spirit and of one mind." It is a transformation worth working on.

The practice of "Clear" requires layers of trust and emotional safety. It requires discernment on the part of leadership. While differences and difficulties might be acknowledged in group meetings at Good Works, they are usually worked through and resolved privately, between the persons involved.

Theology of Failure/Freedom to Fail

A theology of failure is based on realizing that God values and uses our offerings of faith, regardless of the outcome of those efforts. This does not mean excusing intentional negligence, carelessness, or bad behavior. A theology of failure refers to times we have trusted God for initiatives that ultimately don't seem to work out. It involves taking those experiences and learning from them.

Sometimes, when we have done our best in the context of community and have made use of the gifts God has given us, things still don't turn out as we intended them to. And sometimes things go badly. Our motives and intentions are important, and we can learn a lot from failure. If we can make mistakes and not let them seriously damage our lives, but let God work through those mistakes, we can learn about the kingdom of God in ways that success or expertise would not teach us. Failure can be a way to learn what's important to God (2 Cor. 12:9).

Failure can be a way to learn what's important to God

Nevertheless, outcomes matter, and in some situations, mistakes can be very costly. So, in environments where others could be harmed by our mistakes, the risks of failure have to be considered. But if people are going to grow in their innovation and initiative, there must be safety to try things and fail. And from this "freedom to fail" emerge second generation questions— things none of us thought of until we were right in the midst of them, and new challenges and questions came to the surface, requiring new ways to react and respond. It's important to allow room and energy for experiment and change. Some of that energy and wisdom comes from having dealt redemptively with prior failures and from what we have learned when things don't work the way we expected them to.

Leaders can cultivate a robust theology of failure. While we might agree with the adage: "fail often in order to succeed sooner,"[7] it is important to figure out what to do with our fail-

7. IDEO, a consultancy, has coined the slogan "fail often in order

ures. Leaders bear a particular responsibility for the well-being of the community, but they also give permission to others to undertake acts of faith that bring them to maturity. If we can become friends with failure, we can learn and do things previously thought impossible. Often as a person rises higher in the leadership of an organization, he or she grows less and less willing to take risks in order to avoid being seen as having made a significant mistake. But in addition, a leader has increasingly more responsibility over others. One's choices and one's mistakes have a larger impact. But the freedom to innovate, to be spontaneous, to take risks and build something fresh are held in creative tension with possibilities of failure and disappointment.

An Ethic of Inefficiency

A freedom to fail and an ethic of inefficiency intersect when "the process is the product," when how we get to the goal is as important as the goal itself. If something doesn't work out perfectly, we can still trust that God is working in us and shaping us into the body of Christ. "Getting it done" cannot be the highest priority. But arguing for that is risky in a culture that wants clear and measurable results, ever-improving numbers, and dramatic testimonies regarding effectiveness. Some donors and funding sources want numbers—whether it is how many food baskets were distributed at Thanksgiving, or how many people were saved or got jobs.

It is important that people trust the vision, integrity, and spirit with which an organization accomplishes its work. Sometimes statistics are used to justify a ministry, but for Good

---

to succeed sooner," and a similar quotation is credited to Tom Kelley. https://www.economist.com/business/2011/04/14/fail-often-fail-well.

Works, integrity and faithfulness to our mission and to God are the justification, and the numbers are secondary. Nevertheless, an ethic of inefficiency is not an excuse, or an endorsement, for sloppiness.

Within Good Works, there are significant internal organizational structures, and the standards and protocols for the community are high. One staff member noted, "We are quite efficient and effective in getting things done, but numbers and results don't drive the ministry or its evaluation. What is most important is whether people feel loved. Are they experiencing the love of God? Are they treated with dignity and respect? Is hope being communicated? Are people really being cared for here in a way that honors God, honors the people, and opens people's hearts to the love of Christ?"

Much of ministry is accompaniment, walking *with* a person through difficult circumstances. And that is rarely efficient. It is slow and can be painful. In these cases, a focus on efficiency is misplaced; the point is to be there, to suffer *with* the person. While our cultural tendency is to interpret suffering as failure, suffering can be a door through which we come to know Christ more deeply (Phil. 3:10). Sometimes we walk alongside persons as they struggle, and we bear their burdens with them. In other cases, we suffer as our hopes for improvement in someone's life are shattered again and again as they battle addiction, mental health challenges, or difficult circumstances. We grieve, lament, and feel failure when events and choices are out of our control, and seem out of their control. In these places, we can still connect to God, fulfilling what God desires of us—to know him and make him known.

Much of ministry is accompaniment . . . and that is rarely efficient

Other examples of an ethic of inefficiency are the time-intensive approaches Good Works uses in hiring and promoting staff. When someone new wants to explore the possibility of joining the staff of Good Works, there is a multilayered process. He or she is invited to come and spend time informally with the community for several days—in a sense, interviewing the community. The individual is then sent home before being invited back for a formal interview process. After the individual has left after the first visit, coworkers are interviewed to discern together God's will in the situation. This lengthy approach protects staff and recipients and broadens the discernment process to include various parts of the community. It also strengthens the identity of the community as members have a chance to describe and explain their commitments and values in response to the applicant's questions.

This "inefficient" process also comes into play with staff promotions. One of the challenges in promoting people is that we don't know whether they will be trustworthy in a setting in which they will have significant new levels of responsibility or whether they will be able to trust themselves. Promotion is a risk, but at Good Works, the decision is often based on the earlier process of how people joined the community. Many of Good Works' full-time staff were former interns. Watching individuals go through the internship and seeing them troubleshoot things well makes it easier to promote them to new responsibilities.

These processes are also evident in how most long-term volunteers come into the community and in how persons are chosen for other initiatives. The way in which a person is welcomed as a resident in the Timothy House is similarly time intensive. Someone could ask, "You did a half hour phone interview and the person never showed up—isn't this a waste of time?" Not for Good Works. It's part of creating a good community and discerning how to be helpful, and it is viewed as an offering to the Lord.

Leaving Well

Recently there has been much discussion and writing about "finishing well." Sometimes finishing has to do with transitions or assessing a whole life. Often, when a person leaves a staff position, however, there is little attention to finishing well. The church and Christian ministries generally put their energy and emphasis on joining and making commitments. But less frequently is anything said about leaving well, especially when it is under awkward circumstances. When people make commitments, there should be a way to rework them periodically and to end them thoughtfully. Whether things are going well or poorly, departure is not the time to introduce protocols for leaving, but rather at the start. And so Good Works includes a section on leaving well in its employment contracts. Part of the contract includes:

> It is expected that when it comes time to leave the Good Works staff, you will leave well. By this we mean that you will make every effort to leave in right relationships with any coworker, volunteer, or recipient/participant you have met during your time on staff. We take this biblical passage "if it is possible, as far as it depends upon you, be at peace with everyone" (Romans 12:18) to mean that God asks us to cultivate a willing spirit with regard to the hard work of humility, good communication, forgiveness and reconciliation. Leaving well simply means you are agreeing to do your part to bring closure to the relationships formed through your time at Good Works and to transition off the staff with the blessing of the community.

A complicated situation at Good Works illustrates a commitment to making departures as good as possible: for a number of reasons, a long-term staff member was asked to leave. It was a very difficult decision that the leadership had weighed and considered carefully over an extended period of time. Though the immediate departure was abrupt, the community very much wanted to preserve the relationship. This was done by inviting the former staff member back to the community several weeks later for a time of affirmation and appreciation, which was received well.

This is rare in organizations, even when persons are laid off for financial rather than performance issues. Usually the break is total, even when the relationships have been long and deep. And this often causes enormous pain. All of the contributions, sacrifices, and shared efforts are unrecognized by the community, leaving the departing staff member deeply hurt and often very conflicted. The community is also often harmed by not having good closure. Developing protocols for helping staff members leave well, while preserving relationships and valuing shared history, is an expression of faithfulness and integrity on the part of the community or organization.

Conclusion

When we understand that what we do emerges from who we are, and who we are is shaped by what we do and how we do it, we recognize the centrality of integrity to the entire process of formation and discipleship of individuals and communities. Taking short cuts, ignoring warning signs, or thinking we can skip truthfulness "this once" endangers our witness, service, and community life. Although these concerns and commitments can be challenging, it helps to see that all of our efforts at faithfulness and integrity are also expressions of worship of the God who is faithful and true.

An important way we gain a window into a life of integrity is by paying attention to perspective—whether it is God's, a co-worker's, or that of a person who depends on our assistance. Keeping perspective is the focus of the next chapter.

Prayer

Lord, we know that unless you "build the house, the builders labor in vain" (Ps. 127:1). You are the foundation for any good work of ministry, and we thank you that we have been invited into something much bigger than ourselves. Help us to live and serve with faithfulness and integrity.
Amen.

Questions for Reflection and Discussion

1. Have you experienced the presence or absence of integrity in a Christian organization? What has been the result?
2. How do you and your church or community encourage truthful speech in contested circumstances?
3. In your ministry, how have you seen (or missed) opportunities to express trust and respect to the people you help or supervise?
4. What frameworks for accountability have been helpful in your life and community?
5. What ways have you or your community found to address interpersonal and intra-staff conflict? Does your community have a structure for regularly addressing conflict? How could you better protect the unity God has already given to the community?

6.   How is a "freedom to fail" important in your experience or community? How has it opened up new insights and opportunities?

7.   In what ways does less emphasis on efficiency appeal to you or worry you?

8.   Have you seen communities handle difficult departures well? What did that look like?

THREE

Keeping Perspective

Caring for people well begins with seeing them as their Creator sees them. A holy perspective on individuals who may at first seem unlovable stems from our commitment to letting God renew our minds through worship. Only God can give us the grace to see each person as a child of God, made in his image—with dignity, beauty, and purpose.

Desperation and coping strategies for survival often create unhealthy habits, and it is no wonder that some people become quite difficult and demanding. But just as God's grace sees beyond our brokenness to the person we were meant to be, God can give us eyes of grace to see beyond those destructive patterns to the beautiful person God sees. Every individual is both fallen and precious, and created to fulfill God's good purposes on earth. Even when the people who are being served face miserable situations, we can emphasize our common humanity and treat each one with integrity and dignity.

God often uses our own histories, difficulties, disappointments, and need to help us relate to the challenges others face. My (Keith's) perspective and compassion were first shaped by my own experience of lostness and living on the margins of community and the transformation that came through Christian friends and faith in Jesus.

My Story: A Personal Version of Lost and Found

I was raised in a practicing Jewish family and grew up in a Jewish community in Cleveland, Ohio.[1] My father died suddenly when I was twelve, and my mother remarried a few years later. As far as I know, I never met a Christian in the sixteen years I lived in Cleveland. It amazes me that there were churches on almost every corner, so to speak, but I had never met a person who lived out the life of a Christian in a way that got my attention. I was part of an unreached people group—never having seen the witness of someone who lived the life of a follower of Jesus—up until I was sixteen. My family moved from Cleveland to a small town outside of Dayton, Ohio, and I named it the "Land of the Gentiles." I met Christians for the first time through a teacher and a classmate. They began to love me, and so the context of hearing the gospel involved being welcomed and accepted. And I was a jerk, if I may say so myself. I was a drug addict; I spent five years in the drug culture and was pretty difficult to be around. I was a user and had been a dealer while I lived in Cleveland.

I accepted Jesus into my life (only to later understand that he accepted me first) through what was called a "Four Spiritual Laws" booklet and said, "OK, God, if you're real, become real to me." The two Christians I first met remained friends throughout the process and are friends to this day. Strange things began to happen in my life. I noticed things that I had never noticed before. And things that used to bother me no longer bothered me. I was beginning to be bothered by new things. And I was turning into someone that I actually liked! So I decided to read the Bible, and because I hated to read and the chapters looked

---

1. In this chapter, many of the stories are told in Keith's voice. When the personal pronouns *I*, *me*, or *my* are used, they are referring to Keith's particular experiences.

short, I started with the book of "Palms," which only later I fig-
ured out was not called "Palms." I just read a little Scripture every
day and prayed a little; and God and a community used those acts
of faithfulness to shape me into a different kind of person.

The real miracle, though, was that I graduated high school.
It was a monumental event. I hardly went to school after sixth
grade, so I didn't learn much. In my senior
year of high school, I met with the principal
and said to him, "Listen, I became a Christian about a year ago. I'm realizing things
that I never realized before, and I've decided
that I'd like to stay [in school] an extra year." He looked at me like,
"What? Are you crazy? We don't do that here." I was so naive. . . .
Anyway, I had to graduate that year, which was good. I look back
on those years and am thankful that God could still use me, and
if God can use me, God can use anybody. The gift of salvation
was a comprehensive rescue for me.

I was part of an
unreached people group

I went on to Ohio University with a passion to witness to
everything that moved. I had such joy in communicating my
faith—not a lot of knowledge, but a lot of joy. Like Peter and
John say in Acts 4:20, "We cannot help speaking about what we
have seen and heard." And that is where I was. I was just constantly describing how God was working in my life, and it was
wonderful. I found myself drawn to people who didn't fit well
into society, and, eventually, a friend of mine and I enrolled in
a two-year associate's degree program in mental health to add
onto our bachelor's degrees. We wanted to learn about how to
care for people, and we did an internship in a domestic violence
shelter. There the Lord spoke to me—not in words, but in a strong
desire, a dream, about building a place in my basement to care
for people who needed a place to stay. This was four years before
anybody was using the word "homeless." We called them "dis-
placed persons." But the language was not adequate.

With a small inheritance I had received, I had bought a house. I had already read Robert Coleman's book, *The Master Plan of Evangelism*, and I was committed to selecting people to live with me, and together I thought we could try to live out the values from Coleman's book.

In the fall of 1980, we started an outreach to widows in the area, and in January of 1981, we began caring for people without homes. Then Darlene and I were married in September, and she moved into this thing nine months after it began. She was willing, apprehensive, and courageous and brought an invisible strength that created stability. Having other people in the house wasn't unusual for her; it was the way she had been living for several years. As a child, Darlene had experienced poverty and later found it quite natural to interact with people facing similar circumstances. It was another way God prepared us for the Good Works mission. Good Works is the fruit of a good marriage.

The first person who came to stay with us was Carol. Despite my having lived in Athens, Ohio, for the previous five years, I was not very familiar with the area she came from—a place called Appalachia. Or is it Appalaaaachia? I had been inside the bubble of a university campus and knew almost nothing about the larger community. Carol spoke fast in an accent I struggled to understand. I remember having to ask her to repeat herself several times. About the third time, I just stopped asking and did my best to learn from her. It was Carol who opened my eyes to begin to ask questions about the history, values, and needs of this place. It would be years later before I began to see its beauty.

Two years into the work, I was experiencing what anyone would experience. The steam was running out, and I was discouraged. Later I understood that God was allowing adversity to clarify for me the difference between a concern and a calling. In the furnace of adversity, we discern whether God has given us a special grace to do what we think God has called us to do. And if it's not a calling, then we'll move on to something else, and we won't have the grace to persevere. This perseverance is a holy desperation: "Lord, if your Presence does not go with us, do not send us up from here" (Exod. 33:15). And so, I have persevered in this calling of Good Works for four decades now, trying to live out a theology of love and compassion.

Becoming Homeless to Understand

Matthew 9:36 describes how Jesus responded to the crowds that pressed in on him: "He had compassion on them, because they were harassed and helpless, like sheep without a shepherd." It is such a fitting description for many of the people who struggle with homelessness. To understand that experience more fully, one of the spiritual disciplines I have adopted is to spend time on the street.

Since 1989, I have spent several days every few years in different US cities, living among people who are experiencing homelessness. I go to expand my perspective, and perspective is everything. I know that I can be insulated from the reality of pain, uncertainty, and fear that people without homes feel. Despite my daily interactions with people experiencing homelessness, I can lose perspective and become out of touch. The end result of losing perspective is what the prophet Isaiah calls "the pointing finger" (Isa. 58:9). I go to regain perspective and have my reservoir of compassion replenished. In short, I go for a reality check. I go also to learn—learn how to grow in love for my neighbor and create structures and opportunities for others to do the same. I know that experiences of rural and urban homelessness and poverty are not the same, but my time in city shelters and on city streets has illuminated many of the challenges that Good Works staff members and residents experience. The experiences do not have to be identical to be profoundly informative and even life-changing.

Each of my journeys to live among people experiencing homelessness was intended to be incarnational—to experience life from different perspectives. I wanted to share some of the feelings and struggles that accompany life on the street and in shelters. In all my trips, I used my own name and address but did not reveal to anyone that I was not truly homeless.

I am quite aware, of course, that when I take these brief journeys, I am not really without a home. At best, I can only "pretend" to be poor (Prov. 13:7). In reality, *I go to regain perspective and have my reservoir of compassion replenished* I have friends and family who know where I am and who stand available to assist me at any time. I know there are people praying for me during my journey. I know that one phone call can get me out of my situation—and that is the stark and shocking difference I must face every time I leave the people I've met on the streets. I have the power to leave, and they don't. Homelessness at its core is about power and control—the power people have or don't have over their own lives, and the power others have to control them.

For these experiences, I have chosen cities where I don't know much about the services and shelters provided to those who are without homes. I want to learn where the shelters and services are by asking questions and appearing to need assistance. I want to see how I am looked upon and treated and to experience how people react to me. I go to expand my perspective and understanding of the situation people without homes are in. Some of the other reasons I go are the following:

- To understand more fully how people think and feel, so I can love and serve them better. I want to learn how, in a fresh way, to come alongside people experiencing homelessness. As a Christian, I believe that since God became flesh for our world in order to be a bridge for men and women to have a relationship with their Maker, we too must incarnate ourselves into the world of those whom we care about.

- To experience how it feels to be on the receiving end—how it feels to receive help at city missions, from ordinary people, and from the church. This helps me to gain renewed perspective on the feelings of strangers (Exod. 23:9).
- To better understand the challenges from the perspective of the providers, and to develop opportunities for others to serve in ways that are safe, meaningful, and helpful.
- To reevaluate how we are serving people at Good Works—to explore what we may need to change and how to go about doing that. It is easy to assume we know best about how to help people, but I want to understand what people who are without homes see as a way out.

January 2021 marked the beginning of my forty-first year with Good Works. I am aware now more than ever before how these experiences have helped me more fully to understand that those who experience homelessness are human beings made in the image of God—people who in many ways are not much different from myself. Over the years, I have learned that for any of us to understand and help people who are suffering, we must learn how to leave the comfort of our own security and reach out, perhaps incurring some personal risk and pain. As a Christian, I now more fully grasp what Christ Jesus has done for me. I am grateful, and I want to continue to turn my gratitude into godly activism.

Below are more specific insights that came from my time on the street and in shelters and some of the reflections that emerged from those experiences.

Fear

I learned how vulnerable you are and feel when you have no connections with local people—how hard it is to trust people you don't know. With no identification, no money, and no connections, you feel very alone. You begin to realize how easily you can be taken advantage of. In an unfamiliar city, I didn't know the safe sections from the dangerous ones. Having left behind almost all the resources and securities taken for granted in a middle-class life, I was uncomfortably dependent on the kindness of strangers.

Prolonged fear can turn you into someone you don't like and don't want to be with. Once, after I had earned a few dollars, I was alone and confronted by a person who appeared to be homeless and demanded my money. To my surprise, I quickly replied that I didn't have any. I learned that fear can prompt us to lie in order to survive—even when we're committed to truthfulness. I realized that it would be difficult to maintain integrity in these situations and how often lying seems the better choice. I also realized that a few lies could roll into a whole lifestyle of lying. If we want people to tell us the truth, we must make sure there are clear incentives to do so, and that it is safe for them to do so.

I realized that living on the street would change my identity into someone I never wanted to be

I realized that living on the street would change my identity into someone I never wanted to be. I wondered how often this was the case for other folks I encountered. How did they remember themselves before they experienced homelessness? I learned that it is often fear that makes people compromise their own moral standards to survive.

Time and Money

I learned that time can be the enemy of people without homes. For so much of the day, there is nothing to do and nowhere to go. So much idle time to get depressed. So little hope. Yes, you can work your tail off for eight hours at minimum wage, but then you spend each day's income to meet the comfort needs of that day. I learned that it is very difficult to save money when you don't have a stable environment. When you do earn money, you become a target for others to steal from, exploit, or beg you to give to them. This becomes an impossible rut to get out of on one's own. I think it is this sense of hopelessness that tempts some people to medicate themselves to relieve the pain. I also learned how harsh the world looks when you have no money, and how different you feel when you have a few dollars with which to buy a meal. I had not fully understood that before.

Rules

I learned that there are many complicated but unclear rules in shelters. In one case, the rules were eight pages long, single-spaced, and located behind a glass case. There was no time during the intake process to read the rules, but I was expected to sign my name agreeing to obey them. Rules were erratically enforced, sometimes ignored, and other times enforced vigorously without any explanation of the reasoning behind them.

For example, as I walked slowly through a hallway at a shelter, passing the kitchen, I was approached by a staff worker who scolded me for walking through the hall to the chapel. I got the feeling that he thought I was trying to get away with something. I learned that all of the men must leave the building through the back door, go outside, walk around to the front, and enter the chapel by the front door. The idea didn't appear to make much sense, but I decided to follow instructions. Just as I turned to leave, the staff worker told me he would make an exception since I was almost at the chapel anyway. He told me to walk on through. The episode reminded me of how much power workers have in minor interactions.

I assumed there was a reason for this untold and unwritten rule, so I pursued the matter further the next morning with another worker. I was simply told that this was the policy. After three attempts, I still couldn't get staff workers to explain the reason for the rule. I felt treated like a brainless idiot. "I can respect the policy," I thought, "I'm simply interested in the reasoning." I reflected on my own tendency to disregard sincere questions from our residents because they irritated me. It's easy to be on guard against being manipulated and assume the worst about people. I was reminded how I need to take more time to explain the reasoning behind our structures and policies. I wondered about what expectations might be unclear to those who come to Good Works.

The "don't walk through the building" rule was only one example of the many unclear rules and expectations I found during my experiences. That mission, like others I have stayed in, had little to no orientation policy for its new residents. I discovered that rules were more often caught than taught. On several occasions, I found myself in the wrong place—being scolded—but not realizing I was in the wrong. For example, after using the bathroom in one shelter, I was scolded for remaining at the drinking fountain while I read the bulletin board. Later, I was scolded for sitting in the wrong chair during a chapel meeting. There were no signs or posted rules to indicate I was in the wrong. It was frustrating to be scolded frequently for not following rules I didn't know existed.

Power Dynamics

At times, it was hard to tell who was in charge in a shelter. I often wondered whether I was being bossed around to fulfill the personal power needs of another resident or employee. Good communication from the staff to the residents is very important, and how we communicate is as important as what we communicate.

Sometimes workers convey an arrogant attitude of being the expert who, with their expertise, will show us the right way. I wonder whether we can, in humility, instead be "one beggar telling another beggar where to find bread." I think that the real test of the genuineness of our talk about Christ is revealed in the attitude of humility (Phil. 2:3-8).

How we communicate is as important as what we communicate

Manipulation is a way that people who do not have direct or overt power attempt to get what they want or need. People who are caught in desperate circumstances, homelessness, or poverty sometimes turn to it when they are dependent on others. The manipulation can push buttons among the staff who can respond in ways that make the situation worse. I know. I have responded to manipulation in ways that were not helpful.

Some Christian social ministries and missions pride themselves on rejecting government involvement, but then they put a harsh, power-hungry person in charge of the residents. Because of limited budgets for personnel, organizations sometimes rely on their more seasoned clients to manage the newer ones. My most significant experiences of several missions came from the persons with whom I had the most contact, and they were folks who seemed to behave no differently from other men in the shelter. The reliance on persons who found their sense of identity by wielding control over others ended up being the real witness of the mission, and it was not a good one.

Every ministry and staff person faces temptations to misuse power and control, but it is important to acknowledge the temptations and address them. Residents can be given responsibility, but if they are not equipped to face their own needs and brokenness, they can become abusive and exploit the more vulnerable persons who come in. A loss of self-worth can cause people to strive for a position of power through physical threats and intimidation. If the practices of the ministry are being modeled by those who are harsh and unloving, then the ministry loses its power to model the transforming message of freedom and healing in Christ.

In my experience, the real witness of any ministry to people who are experiencing homelessness is not its required worship services but the way in which it fosters or doesn't foster Christian community. Its witness for Christ is demonstrated by the actions, attitudes, and examples of the people whom the administration places in authority over the residents. The man who refused to give me my clothes early one morning demonstrated his need for power and control. He appeared to enjoy the fact that he had the authority to deny me the privilege to leave the shelter when I wanted to.

Humiliation and dehumanization can be daily fare for people without much status. In one shelter, I tried to learn something about their operations and had a series of questions I wanted to ask. I was eventually asked "who I was with," and I replied that I was "with me." The staff person's response suggested that since I was only trying to satisfy my own curiosity, I wasn't worth his time, so to be sure I asked him: "Are you saying that if I am with someone, you will speak with me, but if I'm not, you won't take the time?" "That's right," he said and walked away. I felt dehumanized by the interaction. Later, however, a security guard willingly took me on a tour and explained the program. In another shelter, I asked for permission to use the bathroom. The staff person responded, "I just cleaned it," and his tone of voice sent the message that my use of it would make it dirty. It was humiliating.

Privacy

Privacy is a resource available for purchase by those who have money. The less money you have, the less privacy you can obtain. We need privacy, however, to maintain our mental health. I remember feeling like there was no place to go where I could be by myself. We were always around others who could potentially take advantage of us. When this low-level stress combines with physical sickness or some form of disability, it can make a person behave strangely. No wonder people living on the street sometimes appear to be mentally ill.

Food

Food is the centerpiece of the day for many people who are experiencing homelessness. It provides immediate gratification to numb the pain of the rest of the day. In fact, many of the people I spent time with made meals the event around which they arranged their whole schedule.

Because food is so important, it is a source of power, and sometimes those who control access to food use it as a weapon. One day, I noticed the men picking up brown bags for lunch. I went over to the kitchen and requested a bag but was told that I had to sign up the day before for such a bag. No one had ever told me that, and there were no rules posted regarding this requirement. I was again reminded of how important it is to explain things to our residents both verbally and in writing, and to apologize when we have failed in our responsibility to communicate well. I was again reminded that the "system" often seems cold and uncaring.

On a more recent trip, I became overwhelmingly aware of how difficult it is to eat nutritious food on a regular basis, because most of the food that's donated is high in carbohydrates, saturated fat, sodium, and sugar and long in shelf life. Once, I arrived in the cafeteria to discover that everyone was having the same breakfast: Froot Loops with sugar on top and coffee. I followed the group and had a heavy dose of white sugar. I had

had many similar breakfasts in shelters over the years. Now struggling with diabetes myself, I wondered how many of the men had little choice but to eat food that was really bad for them. It helped me realize the importance of getting nutritious food to people whom we're helping.

Work

I discovered that sometimes the shelter system is at odds with working. One time, I found myself with about twenty men in a small beat-up building, sitting and waiting for work. I read the very old signs on the walls. I learned that if you wanted work, you had to be there to apply at around 6:30 a.m. You would be paid minimum wage and return to the city at 4:00 p.m. This meant that the men who worked that shift would not be back in time to get a bed at the shelter, which required that they line up at 2:00 p.m. Why would a shelter make rules that conflicted with regular work arrangements?

Another time—in one of my earliest experiences—I got a day job stripping tobacco. I went with several other guys from the shelter. I found it to be hard and unpleasant work. I began to think about all those sermons I had heard, believed, and even repeated on the subject of excellence. I remember thinking that a good witness is one who does good work. But I felt weak and tired. It was hard to strive for excellence. I looked over and saw the other men from the shelter working hard and not stopping except for an occasional smoke. I thought to myself, "Here I am, a Christian director of a ministry with people experiencing homelessness, looking for an excuse to stop work while these men next to me are not complaining, speaking evil of the work, or taking breaks." It certainly was an eye-opening experience. I realized that I had much less stamina for hard labor than many of these men. They were far from lazy and, in many ways, much more motivated than I was.

That day, I started to feel sick and very tired from a bad night's sleep in the shelter, but I also realized that much of my energy was being sapped by the physical working environment and the emotional abuse from the boss. I decided that I had to focus my thoughts in some constructive direction, so I turned them to my wife, my home, my job, and my friends. I tried to cling to those things that gave my life meaning. I felt better for a moment but then realized that the men I was working with did not have many of these things to strengthen them. I was renewed by a whole new sense of gratitude for what I had so often taken for granted, but also felt like I was starting to understand emotionally— though only in a small way—what it was like to have no home.

Loss of Identity

During the very first time I went into a city to experience what it was like to be without a place, after walking around for forty-five minutes and becoming lost, I realized that people were looking at me differently. Was it because of what I was wearing or because my walking didn't seem to have a destination? Their looks started to sap my energy. I wondered whether they were wondering, "What's wrong with him? Is he mentally ill? Why doesn't he get a job?" The looks didn't take me down immediately because I still felt strong and emotionally secure, but I started to realize how quickly a person's sense of identity and self-worth can be crushed.

I realized that people were looking at me differently. . . . Their looks started to sap my energy

When we lose a sense of who we are, we also lose the realization of the image of God within us and question our purpose in this world. As people lose connections with family, work, and love, identity is undermined. We become vulnerable to the seduction of a new identity, the identity of a bum or a street person—unattached to any network of accountability that fosters human integrity and growth. I was reminded again of how important it is for people who have experienced homelessness to leave behind that identity.

Faith

I did not find much antagonism toward Christianity among the men I met. In fact, I found a real respect for—and openness to—Jesus. I sensed that many of the men knew he was real and was willing to listen to their prayers. At some point in their lives, many seemed to have made a decision to follow Christ, but their options and choices of social community had held them back from fully living for and following him.

I also thought about why so many middle-class churches have so much trouble integrating people who are experiencing poverty into their social communities. Maybe the gospel has yet to penetrate our classism. Why are class and race not even issues in many discussions of extending the gospel to people who are poor? What are the obstacles in my lifestyle and in the lifestyle of my coworkers in the church? Am I blind, too? Must people who want to follow Jesus first become middle-class to be welcomed into most churches? How can the church reach out and build bridges rather than walls?

One time, I attended a worship service in a church that "welcomed the homeless" and celebrated their changed lives. I participated in the singing and prayers. When the service was over, the people began to file out of the pews and into the hallway. Every person who passed me ignored my presence. Not even a hello; the lack of acknowledgment saddened me deeply. I felt ignored and avoided. My experience brought to mind the words in James 2:2–4:

> Suppose someone comes into your meeting wearing a gold ring and fine clothes, and a poor person in filthy old clothes also comes in. If you show special attention to the one wearing fine clothes and say, "Here's a good seat for you," but say to the one who is poor, "You stand there" or "Sit on the floor by my feet," have you not discriminated among yourselves and become judges with evil thoughts?

In many Christian missions to people experiencing homelessness, there is a requirement that a person attend a sermon or chapel service in exchange for food and shelter. This seems to run contrary to the free grace we proclaim. If we are going to require anything, why not state clearly that persons who are staying at the shelter must meet one-on-one with a trained representative of the organization to discuss their circumstances if they want to stay for more than a few days? This could help a person *Surely, if the gospel really is good news, it is good news for sinners and the sinned against* who is experiencing homelessness face some of his or her problems in an atmosphere of personal caring and accountability. Not once during my eleven times staying in shelters was I ever asked to meet with anyone to discuss why I was homeless.

I remember attending one mandatory chapel service where the preacher gave what I would call a typical "worm" sermon. We all were made to feel like worms. According to him, the sins that we faced were exclusively personal and private. If we would clean up our acts and turn to Christ, our lives would change. While this may be true, this message is not the whole truth. The preacher made it all seem so simple and easy. I wondered whether he had any idea of what these men really faced. Any questions about difficulties arising from low-paying employment, high-cost housing, dependence on the vagaries of public assistance, impact of prior incarcerations, and the fatherless families many of them came from were answered with an overly simplistic theology that "God is in control, and he does what he wants." It felt as if the preacher was saying, "Tough luck." The message was another "you are on the wrong side of the Lord" sermon. "All of your problems result from not following Christ; follow Christ and all of your problems will be solved." When this message is repeated regularly with little social support available, it invites cynical and despairing responses. Surely, if the gospel really is good news, it is good news for sinners and the sinned against.

I continue to struggle with the methods of ministry I see in the homeless mission system. I wrestle with whether people are invited into a performance or a community. Would any of us who are not homeless be comfortable with being required to attend a worship service in order to get something we needed from the church? I find that these requirements are counterproductive in working with people who have no place to live. Instead, what if we arranged to hold our fellowship meetings at a time and place accessible to people in our shelter and simply invite them to join what we are already doing? This way, our meetings are not a performance but simply an expression of who we are. Maybe the real ministry is letting those who are poor or without homes see us as we are—and gathered for worship. Maybe their presence would shape our discipleship. Maybe it is as much about our social lives as our spiritual lives.

More in Common Than Expected

After several days in one city, as I was laughing and telling jokes with a number of the men from the shelter, I realized how much these men longed for the same things I did: deep and trusting human relationships where they felt cared for, work that would provide dignity and a decent living wage, and emotional affirmation for who they were as human beings. They longed for a place to call home where they could be themselves, live in peace, and use their own resources to help others. I sensed that some of these men would welcome a right relationship with God and their neighbors if they experienced a social structure in which they could maintain good relationships. I also wondered what might happen to me and my close friends if we were thrust into the circumstances these men faced. Would our faith hold if we were forced to survive on the streets?

> *Would our faith hold if we were forced to survive on the streets?*

Trust

I learned how important trust is, especially in a context of fear, and how a staff person's small accidental mistakes or misleading information about timing, resources, or locations can have difficult results for the person dependent on the information. One time, a staff person indicated that he felt bad about accidentally misleading me, and I appreciated his sensitivity to my situation. It increased my trust for him, and I was reminded of how important establishing trust was in our own ministry.

Street living can be very unpredictable. Sometimes a friend you've made later turns on you unexpectedly; other times friends leave you without any notice and never come back. Such uncertainty in relationships affects any sense of trust. The issue is similar for those of us who want to help people who are without a home. We must bring a sufficiently large emotional bank account to the relationship so that we can withstand emotional and psychological withdrawals. It is important to have a firm grasp on the process of giving and receiving forgiveness, and to be in touch with our own unresolved conflicts. Otherwise, we will turn our unresolved bitterness and resentments toward the person who is experiencing homelessness when he or she pushes our buttons.

Some of the people we work with do not respond well to efforts at intervening in their lives. Like injured puppies, people can bite when someone tries to help. Reaching out to people who have experienced rejection, pain, and abuse will cause us to be stretched to our limits. Hurting people can "spill" their pain onto us when we bump into each other. When they walk away, we are often left bruised. When individuals can't face the fact that they are angry and disappointed with themselves, sometimes they direct their anger and manipulation toward those who want to help. Others appear to have arranged their lives in ways that allow them to ignore their own responsibilities and to always place the blame on someone else.

Sometimes, people's pain speaks so loudly that they can't hear or understand our message no matter who says it or how it is presented. Not everyone who is in emotional or physical pain is able to hear and quickly understand the Lord's unfailing love for them and their need to respond personally. When Moses brought to the Israelites the great news that God would deliver them from slavery, they didn't respond with gratitude or joy. The writer says, "they did not listen to him [Moses] because of their discouragement and harsh labor" (Exod. 6:9). Some people need a ministry of presence that simply seeks to be with them and slowly helps them return to a place where they can even hear again. Sometimes trust is built very slowly over time.

The Problem Continues

I learned that while there are many good and caring people on the front lines of helping those without homes, the problem of homelessness doesn't seem to be getting much better. I stayed in a city with an estimated three thousand homeless people. I went from shelter to shelter looking for a bed. Only by God's grace was I able to find a place to sleep. Homelessness continues to be the result of a collision of personal vulnerabilities and choices and societal systems beyond an individual's control. People experiencing homelessness are caught in a quagmire of broken relationships and social injustices combined with the learned coping habits of survival that often do not help them escape poverty.

The Role of Others in Maintaining Perspective

Life-changing ministry with hurting and abused people is impossible outside the context of community. The very nature of that work brings us into contact with some very draining people—individuals who, because of the ways they deal with pain, can drain us of our life and energy. And unless we establish emotional boundaries and obtain from the Lord a balanced self-esteem, we are destined to ride a roller coaster of emotions and hurt that can produce bitterness, resentment, and eventually depression.

In community, we can bear one another's burdens, share vital information, and hand over to one another the most difficult people while we take time for refreshment. In community, we can maintain a relational checks-and-balances system whereby we are able to say to one another, "Don't you think you are losing perspective and that you were too harsh with that person?" In community, we help each other understand how to recover from the emotional pain inflicted by hurting people. In community, we can choose the most loving response and teach and model dignity and responsibility and learn to prevent burnout.

One staff member described a difficult experience:

As I was ending my shift at the Timothy House one evening, I asked about the well-being of a resident who had been working almost nonstop while also enduring chronic pain. He was sitting by himself in the kitchen, and I asked him, "How is your knee today?" He answered, "Don't pretend like you care. It doesn't become you." After coming up with some reply like "I'm sorry that you don't believe that I care, I really do," I went into the back office and, in tears, told a coworker about the interaction. He was concerned about me and the resident who was clearly dealing with a lot of pain. The entire staff that week came alongside me to help me not believe that lie, but even with their support it was hard to recover from the blow. Were it not for their encouragement, a seed of bitterness would have consumed me. Later, after he moved out and found greater stability in his work and health, the former resident stopped by one day to thank the staff for the services they had provided. Though he and I never reconciled personally, over time I have come to see that the accusation, though directed toward me, was not even about me. Thank goodness for coworkers who were able to persevere in loving this hurt individual when I was too wounded to do so.

At Good Works, perspective is maintained in several other ways. A number of the senior staff know what it is like to experience homelessness, as they began their relationship with Good Works as residents of the shelter. Sometime later they joined the staff. These coworkers are crucial in fulfilling the mission and vision. They bring a distinctive understanding and perspective based in experience and add credibility to the ministry. And other staff members listen to them.

Perspective is also kept by regular checkups—internal and external—by insiders and outsiders. For example, because of

Good Works' relationship with a local university and especially with their volunteer program, the school provides checks. Such scrutiny is very valuable; Good Works does not view it as a burdensome intrusion. We have also recognized how important it is to learn from the questions people ask. Especially helpful are interns' questions that cause us to look at our everyday practices and assumptions in fresh ways.

Another element in keeping perspective is the desire to do so, since it is easy to become intoxicated with success and attention. It is important to have enough sense of perspective that attention from the media and other groups doesn't distract from the mission. Perspective is also helped by listening for prophetic voices that move us out of the tunnel vision that can plague organizations. Those voices can return us to our original commitments. Our own mission and vision statements are a guard rail in keeping perspective and staying on track—they remind, guide, and clarify.[2]

Taking Seriously God's Perspective

Think again about Jesus's words in Matthew 25: "I was hungry and you gave me something to eat . . . a stranger and you invited me in." Now, imagine eight or ten doors in a hallway. Each door opens into a room—or into the needs and opportunities provided by a relationship with a hungry, sick, or lonely person. When you walk through the "stranger and you invited me in" door, you see other doors, and they are the back entrances to all the other rooms in the hallway. When you enter one relationship or one

2. Good Works uses the Carver Policy Governance Model. See https://www.carvergovernance.com/model.htm.

situation, you often realize there is much more going on than what you first saw. So, you assess what you can do, but often it also opens into more opportunities for relationship, helping, friendship, and ministry.

So often people wonder where to begin in responding to God's concern for the vulnerable. The three groups already identified from Scripture—orphans or fatherless children, widows, and strangers—are excellent starting places. We don't need a grand vision; we simply need to begin. In the covenant with Israel, God is described as the one who "executes justice for the orphan and the widow, and who loves the strangers" (Deut. 10:18 NRSV). Job, a model of faithful living, describes his own practices:

> I rescued the poor who cried for help, and the fatherless who had none to assist them. Those who were dying blessed me; I made the widow's heart sing. I put on righteousness as my clothing; justice was my robe and my turban. I was eyes to the blind and feet to the lame. I was a father to the needy; I took up the case of the stranger. I broke the fangs of the wicked and snatched the victims from their teeth. (Job 29:12–17)

These groups also represent the people who are marginalized in almost every society: those most likely to be lonely, vulnerable, economically in need, and often cut off from their biological families. The fatherless or orphan is the child who is often not tied to healthy adult relationships—one who is experiencing the risks of poverty. The widow or widower is the woman or man who has lost a spouse or is facing disability or aging with limited family support. The alien or stranger is the person who has few good connections with a community, sometimes leading to homelessness.

Most of the "orphans, widows, and strangers" in the Good Works community are from Southeast Ohio, and their struggles are varied. Job loss, relocation, or domestic disputes have caused some to lose their homes. There are veterans, students, single parents, teens aging out of foster care, and those recently released from prison. Some are dealing with emotional distress, mental illness, addictions to sex, food, alcohol, opiates or other drugs, or unhealthy relationships. Others are living with various kinds of disability, have experienced abuse or violence, are caught in legal troubles, or have been stuck in poverty for a long time. Many are struggling with some level of disconnection from family and friends and lack an adequate support system. Systemic issues contribute to their vulnerability. The lack of education and the severe shortage of affordable housing, meaningful employment, and transportation in the area are barriers faced by nearly everyone. Often, it is when several of the above factors collide that people find themselves in an overwhelming crisis.

As much as people who are poor or without homes might need our help, equally so, we the body of Christ need them. While sometimes we might wonder, "God, why did you send this person to me? I can't help them," it is in these times we might hear God whisper, "I know, I have sent them to help you." If our goal is to know Christ and to make him known, then Jesus will reveal himself to us as we respond to "the least of *"I made the widow's heart sing"* these." A deeper relationship with God is available as we "spend" ourselves (Isa. 58:10) into the lives of those in economic, physical, and social need. As we grow in God's perspective, and as we understand better the experiences of the people with whom we are building relationships, we bring, embody, and experience the good news of Jesus.

Conclusion

Gaining and maintaining perspective is crucial in efforts to live faithfully and wisely. Within a community of friends, we find some of the help we need to grow and mature in perspective, wisdom, and grace. A life of worship, and a commitment to integrity, love, and justice are best pursued with others. To the importance of community, we now turn.

Prayer

Lord, help us to see. Help us to see people as you see them—
made in your image with dignity, value, and purpose.
Give us your eyes and your heart to respond in ways that bring
life to others. Help us to see people as you see them, so that
we may learn to love as you love.
Amen.

Questions for Reflection and Discussion

1. What experiences in your life have shaped your perspective on people facing difficult life circumstances?
2. How do you think Keith's own story prepared him for the work he leads?
3. What stood out to you about Keith's times of being on the street? Identify a few of the insights or experiences he shared that really struck or challenged you. Discuss why.
4. Have you seen or experienced life-giving mission/ministry to people who are poor or without homes? What characteristics stood out to you?

5. How could your church or community improve how it responds to people who ask for assistance?
6. In what situations have you learned the importance of community for doing challenging work?
7. How have particular events or experiences in your community or congregation changed your perspective on responding to strangers?

FOUR

A Community of Friends

When Jesus asks us to give ourselves fully to him, does that really include everything? If we imagine that what we do with our careers, money, and choice of spouse matters to God, does God also have a claim on our social lives? When we pray, "Your kingdom come on earth as it is in heaven," are we thinking that God might care about who our friends are?

"Laying down our social lives" as an expression of Christian discipleship and mission is an unfamiliar idea. We generally feel free to choose our friends—mostly if we like them and if they are like us. We reserve our Saturday nights and down time for them. And those choices rarely intersect with our notions of ministry.

We often say that we care about the poor—but what are their names?

We often say that we care about the poor—but what are their names? In social ministry settings, we sometimes view people as projects. But what if God is saying, "I have not given you projects who are poor. I have given you friends"? So these friends become gifts to us, gifts through whom we experience glimpses of the kingdom of God. Perhaps the most life-changing act we could do this week is to sit down and eat with someone not like us.

Did you ever notice how little we truly impact people apart from sharing our lives with them—especially those parts of our lives that we usually reserve for ourselves? Jesus's choices challenge us in the formation of friendships. He was often willing to be friends with people who lived on the margins of the community or who were not respectable by societal standards. He shared his life with disciples whose social standing was questionable, had long conversations and significant friendships with women who were usually overlooked, and cared deeply about persons who were considered unclean by the culture. He gave them his attention and shared the deepest parts of his identity with them.

The apostle Paul also understood the value of personal relationships in transforming lives. In 1 Thessalonians 2:8, he wrote: "Because we loved you so much, we were delighted to share with you not only the gospel of God but our lives as well." It is not enough to share the good news, or our skills and resources; we must learn also to share ourselves.

We often struggle with knowing how the Christian community can express true compassion to neighbors who are struggling with homelessness and poverty. If part of the difficulty they face is a lack of social connections, then substantial healing will come only as we can offer a new community, and that comes by opening our lives to forming new friendships. Until we intentionally make room in our own social networks for those who might seem as if they have little to offer (Luke 14:12), the church will remain powerless in addressing homelessness. Compassion is not a calling; it often involves a choice to lay down our social lives. Unless there is a way for people who are experiencing homelessness to exchange social communities often associated with drugs, theft-for-survival, and sex-on-demand for new relationships, they will stay there a long time. Followers of Jesus can offer life-giving friendships in community.

Many traditional social-work agencies discourage the formation of friendships between clients and providers, but the approach at Good Works is decidedly different. A staff member at Good Works explains,

> A willingness to lay down your social life is not a formal re-
> quirement for staff members, but it is a practice that is mod-
> eled and encouraged. When observed, it is celebrated. In the
> hiring process, staff members look for individuals who want
> to lead this kind of life. We resist the notion that after we
> have put in our weekly work time, we totally leave relation-
> ships behind—in a sense, escaping to find our own space and
> friends. While having other friends and leisure time is im-
> portant, building community and becoming friends with
> former residents is life-giving. It also anticipates more equal
> roles, and for true friendship to develop, it cannot be a rela-
> tionship of permanent dependency. So learned behaviors of
> helplessness or of helping indiscriminately are challenged,
> and friendships can grow into a deeper mutuality.

Often as a way to show compassion, churches engage in a wide range of relief work, meeting immediate needs, but rarely do they move beyond that to addressing the root causes of those needs. And rarely do we consider the importance of disciple-ship or friendship with the people we are helping. Programs and budgets tend to reflect these priorities. But friendship and fellowship—which can't be easily quantified—may be among the very best things we can offer to someone wanting to escape homelessness or gain freedom from addictions.

Forming Friendships in Community

Because of the healing and forgiveness we have found in Jesus, we want our words and actions to draw others to this same source. One staff person comments,

For Good Works, the core motivation is not to solve a so-cial problem or to "fix" people; it is to worship God through love and care for others. One way this is practiced is by inviting folks into our networks of relationships. Sharing a meal, watching a movie, playing basketball, or going to a church event together can be starting places. And we all need starting places. When people who feel unloved or are disconnected from family and friends begin to form healthy relationships with Christian believers, they are often also drawn closer to God.

Another staff member at Good Works explains,

We have developed a practice of inviting those we are learn-ing to love into our regular gatherings of worship—inten-tional times when the community seeks to offer praise and thanks to God and to receive sustaining grace. So, we simply invite our friends into what we are already doing; we would gather whether they came or not. We do not meet to put on a performance for others. Instead, it is a meeting of the body, where together we can experience freedom and truth as we encounter the living God. It is a place of vulnerability and honesty, a place where those we are including can see us for who we really are. When what we say about our lives holds true in our actions, we become credible witnesses of Jesus.

She continues,

Community is not so much about whether we live in the same house or neighborhood as it is about the quality of our connectedness. The extent to which we are in healthy relationships with one another, how we affirm and encour-age, correct and rebuke, apologize and say "I forgive you" . . .

become a testimony to those who are watching us. Being a people who care for, comfort, and confront one another and spur one another toward growth as disciples marked by humility is a powerful form of witness. Nurturing teachable spirits allows us to hear from one another the truth about ourselves, our circumstances, and God. This helps others hear the truth about themselves.

Right and reconciled relationships with one another as staff members or as part of a congregation come prior to any mission of serving people in need. A lifestyle of reconciliation is the credibility we need to speak into the lives of those whose poverty and crisis situations have often been at least partially caused by broken relationships. Without a practice of reconciliation in our community, the impact of ministry outward will be weak at best and harmful at worst.

A Continuum of Relationships across Social Differences

Associating ——*Serving* ——*Loving* ——*Knowing*

But how do we find these new friends? And where do we begin? We can view the formation of friendship on a continuum from most distant to closest relationship. It can start with *associating*, embracing the exhortation in Romans 12:16: "Do not be proud, but be willing to associate with people of low position. Do not think you are superior." We might quickly respond that we do not view folks as "of low position," but often there are people who make us uncomfortable because they are different from us; they don't live in our neighborhoods or go to our favorite coffee shops, and we hesitate to associate with them. We don't know them, and we're not sure we want to. Let's imagine that Paul is challenging us to "hang out together," to put ourselves in places and contexts where our lives might intersect with theirs, places where others might identify us as one of them. It takes work, it takes humility, it takes a bit of dying to self. But we can pray that God will open up connections so that friendships can begin to develop.

A next expression of relationship might involve *serving*. Here there are connections among persons, but the connections often depend on events, programs, or projects with defined roles and time commitments. We go into a relationship by offering people something that they need or by creating an activity that brings people together. We help with a Habitat project or volunteer in a ministry with troubled kids once a week for a few months. As Christians, we choose to serve, to help others, because Jesus has helped us. However, in a relationship that is entirely defined as helper and recipient, at some point we will plateau, move on to something else, or go deeper.

Perhaps we'll choose to go deeper into *loving* the person. This is where everything can get messy. We become engaged emotionally; people surprise or disturb us, and we find ourselves in the challenging position of learning how to truly love a neighbor. We don't necessarily know what to say or how to respond. Our formerly tidy categories become more confused. As we learn of the person's family life, or as we discover that the person doesn't really want our friendship, our self-doubts grow. Loving is very messy, and sometimes we find that maintaining a certain degree of distance is more appealing. The *serving* role is so much more defined and often feels safer. But in loving, we are beginning to really share life with the person. This is a challenging stage, and the awkwardness can last for a while, especially when we are connecting with people quite different from ourselves. If we are going to persevere, it often helps to have another person alongside us, who can say, "Yes, this is difficult, but you can stay with it. I've been there, I know how it feels."

If we are able to move forward in the relationship, we can move to *knowing*. Here there is mutuality in ways we don't often see even in *loving*. In *knowing*, we recognize, "Oh, wow, these people are a gift, there's something here for me too!" And this is where we discover the joy in laying down and opening up our social lives, the joy in experiencing glimpses of the kingdom of God. Relationships don't usually mature to this extent in the midst of a crisis (e.g., of homelessness), but in friendships that are sustained after the crisis has been resolved.

Of course, there are struggles on the path to both *loving* and *knowing*. We often find ourselves saying, "Lord, I may be able to serve these people, and I want to love them, but please don't ask me to become friends with them. I don't even like them. I don't think I can love these people, Lord. Their lives are too much for me. Please let me finish and go home." Nevertheless, God will work through this maturing process, making us into disciples who will deny ourselves and "lose our lives" in order to find them. As we recognize our inability to do this on our own, God gives the power to persevere in love with folks who are sometimes ungrateful and unresponsive. And God gives grace to press on with those who sometimes use manipulation as the door to friendship because that is what they have learned in past relationships.

> *"Lord, I may be able to serve these people, and I want to love them, but please don't ask me to become friends with them"*

With the encouragement of brothers and sisters and the direction of the Holy Spirit, God can bring each of us through this awkwardness toward true friendships that are growing in openness, trust, and mutual transparency. In this context of learning and growth, we can also more easily discern the appropriate time to "speak up for those who cannot speak for themselves," "take up the case of the stranger," or "seek justice" for those who have been oppressed.[1] This may sound like all of the work is on one side of the relationship, but of course that is not true. While most people want to help others, it is important to remember that those "others" also face challenges in loving us in all our peculiarities, missteps, ignorance, and arrogance.

Moving beyond what is comfortable to become friends with people who are different from us is an aspect of discipleship, a way the kingdom of God is revealed in us, to us, and to the world. If God has chosen the poor to be rich in faith and heirs of the kingdom (James 2:5), then there is much about the kingdom to be discovered in our relationships with people who are experiencing forms of poverty and loss. Of course, it takes time. Of course, it can be disorienting, but in these relationships of mutual care and growth, we each learn about fidelity, responsibility, and love. We discover something of the kingdom of God we could not experience in a Bible study or church meeting. A former staff member describes how his view changed:

> I came to Good Works fresh from seminary. Jesus was in my suitcase, and all the answers were in my hands. However, it didn't take participating in very many Friday Night Life gatherings for me to realize that the people I had come to help had a lot to offer me. It is an eye-opening experience for anyone who imagines that giving and growing in relationships happens in one direction only.

Certain aspects of life at Good Works make building friendships across differences more likely. As noted earlier, some staff members were themselves formerly homeless and recipients of help from Good Works. Staff salaries are modest, so income levels are not out of sync with towns nearby. A significant number

1. See Proverbs 31:8; Job 29:12–17; Isaiah 1:17.

of staff members grew up in the area. A general staff commitment to simplified lifestyles reduces class barriers and helps in encouraging commonality.

Seeking Unity within Community

Resentment and bitterness corrupt communities, while being in reconciled and right relationships is key to the Holy Spirit's work in us as a body. In Ephesians 4:1-6, we read that God has already given us unity; it is a gift, and it is our responsibility to maintain it through the work of humility, gentleness, patience, forgiveness, and bearing with one another in love.

When we grow in unity, our restored relationships have a purpose that is beyond ourselves. In his final prayer, Jesus spoke about this clearly:

> "My prayer is . . . that all of them may be one, Father, just as you are in me and I am in you. May they also be in us, so that the world may believe that you have sent me. I have given them the glory that you gave me, that they may be one as we are one—I in them and you in me—so that they may be brought to complete unity. Then the world will know that you sent me and have loved them even as you have loved me." (John 17:20-23)

Unity among the followers of Jesus, then, is a powerful witness. Through our unity in Christ, the world can know and believe that the Father has sent Jesus.

While unity requires a robust practice of forgiveness, it does not wash away or wash out differences or demand that every person view everything similarly. For example, some inside the Good Works community have different perspectives on what solidarity with people in poverty means for their own lives. As one person noted, "We are united by our mission, not by agreeing about everything." Not all Christian communities will look the same, but with reconciled relationships, each will reveal Jesus.

Unity is built on reconciliation. It is sustained by hope in God's ongoing work and faithfulness. And unity also requires integrity. Without it, our claims or efforts at unity become very problematic and are often used to cover over unresolved issues and unaddressed hurts.

Just as God desires to be in reconciled relationship with broken humanity, so human beings are given the ministry of reconciliation. A staff member explains,

> Jesus's teaching in the Sermon on the Mount reminds me that if I am presenting my gift at the altar and remember that a brother or sister is upset with me, I need to act. This is where the practice of humility comes in. So you go to the person and sometimes you know what you have done, but sometimes you don't, and in humility you need to ask. The point is that we will do this before we worship God, because this too is part of worship. If I don't take care of horizontal relationships, I won't be able to pursue the vertical one. A second part of reconciliation is intentionally loving people who haven't sinned against you, but against another person. Our role is to be reconcilers and to facilitate reconciliation for the sake of unity. This is the route to the unity Jesus prays for in the Gospel of John.

Friendship over Time

Loving well—over time—occurs best in the context of community. It is often painstakingly slow. Although living and working together in community is often idealized from the outside, it is both difficult and joy filled. Despite the challenges, it is the soil in which transformative relationships can grow. When relationships, rather than programs, are at the center, "getting it done" is not the priority. Jesus's ministry was not particularly efficient, and the people he engaged were not projects; they became friends.

Initial encounters at Good Works often involve washing dishes together. When we chose from the very beginning not to have dishwashers, the expectation was that the people living and working in the Timothy House would do dishes together (residents, staff, and volunteers), forming new relationships over something each person had to do for the sake of others. "Doing with" can help us grow toward "being with."[2]

The process of developing friendships at Good Works often looks like this: While someone is without a home and working through the issues that have brought them to that place and to their need for Good Works, the level of relationship with staff persons is somewhat limited and structured. But after things have been worked out and the person has left the defined structures of the organization, the possibilities of real mutuality can increase significantly. We encourage this with folks who remain in the area as a way of sharing life together—building relationships that are mutual and last over time. Our "Friday Night Life" gatherings encourage former residents to come back every Friday night to join with staff, volunteers, local church members, neighbors, college students, and seniors for a meal,

When relationships, rather than programs, are at the center, "getting it done" is not the priority

2. Good Works has created specific contexts to encourage growth in mutuality and maturity. They are described in the appendix.

conversation, and special programs. It has been ongoing since 1993 and is a time of weekly celebration and connection.

Over the years, the community has learned that when we don't know someone, it is often best to start at arm's length and bring the person into relationships slowly. It's not helpful to start cheek-to-cheek and then have to push someone away. If we begin slowly, we can stand back and observe and then pray, "Lord, help us to discern where you want us to come into this relationship." It might end up being only a "do for" relationship. We may want it to move into a "do with," but the other person shows us that he or she is not ready, and therefore we can't move forward either.

There are signals that indicate relationships are potentially problematic or have significant risks. One indicator would be if the relationship develops too fast. We don't need to rush into them. If individuals live at the Timothy House for three months in a defined structure, we get to know them. We learn about their existing relationships and how they function in them; we pay attention to how they talk about other people. If there is a lot of blaming and no taking of responsibility, that's a signal. If everyone else is always wrong, and they are always right, that's a warning sign too.

Change happens slowly, but the momentum of progress in one area of life often produces positive change in other areas

Individuals are responsible for their choices and must make an effort to address the situation they are in. The role of the Good Works community is to help people understand what they *can* do and what resources are already available to them. This means the community comes alongside them to encourage, motivate, and empower. Loving accountability is necessary to help folks complete the goals they want to accomplish. Change happens slowly, but the momentum of progress in one area of life often produces positive change in other areas. Having structures in place that allow friendships to develop slowly and grow over time is important and often bears good fruit. A staff member, who had himself been a resident at the Timothy House years earlier, describes his experiences with three young men he met through Good Works:

> Many children grow up in the foster care system, never really having a lifelong family for support. The Timothy House receives many of these "orphaned" young adults. After they turn eighteen and leave foster care, many struggle to make it on their own. Several years back we welcomed three young men who had all lived together at a local residential facility. The Timothy House gave these guys some structure and a place to live while in transition. They shared many experiences together, from struggling with addiction to not feeling like they belonged anywhere. They became very close, like brothers, and some of the Good Works staff invited them to participate in a Celebrate Recovery program and Life's Healing Choices classes. These guys found a place to belong together in community. They began growing and keeping each other accountable.
>
> It's amazing to see God at work in them. Today all three are in different places. One is married and has been blessed with a family of his own. He is in the process of building his own home and is doing well. The second struggled a lot with anger, but he has been employed in various jobs for about two years and has kept a place to live and continues in his recovery family. The third guy moved away to help his pastor start a church in New York, where he was adopted into a family. He has a good job and lets us know how he is doing on occasion. All three are still in my life today in one way or another.

Guardrails for Complex Friendships

In settings where relationships are slowly moving from provider-recipient to mutual friendship, certain guardrails can be very helpful. The first is "dying to the need to be appreciated." Sometimes recipients can be so angry and despairing that they direct their pain toward themselves in the form of self-destructive behavior or express it toward others or toward property. They can respond with antagonism when an effort is made to address the patterns that hold them back from making needed changes. Some are deeply angry because of the injustices that have brought them to the point of requiring help.

Our love, empowered by the Holy Spirit, must learn to endure this anger or despair. One vital step in this process is to confront our own need to be appreciated, and to let it die. This can only happen because we serve people as an expression of worship to God. But, as noted earlier, we need wisdom to discern the boundary between enduring love and tolerating abuse. We can expect to face hardship and be challenged in our emotions and spirits. All service requires some measure of sacrifice, but that is different from allowing staff members, interns, or volunteers to experience abuse from those they are serving. Keeping our relationships open to the input of others is essential. When our emotional involvement in people's lives causes us to lose perspective, we need our brothers and sisters to speak with us and to offer wisdom.

A second guardrail is "keeping it in the light"—a form of horizontal discipleship. Here's an example from Good Works: A resident is moving out of the Timothy House because he or she has found stable housing. A staff person or volunteer wants to stay in relationship with that person. The practice of "keeping it in the light" means that the staff person, intern, or volunteer needs to get permission or a blessing from coworkers to continue the relationship outside of the formal Good Works structure. Usually permission is given, but they are often asked, "tell us why." A staff member explains,

> We don't want control that is heavy handed, but we do want to be kept informed. It's not that we're asking for a report every week, but we do want to be part of the relationship with them. As higher and higher levels of trust develop, this becomes less important. But we want to start out that way because we know there are danger points. We try to discern ways that involve accountability without being overly legalistic.

Recognizing that there are risks, and that sometimes folks try to take advantage of each other (residents, staff, or volunteers), Good Works has developed further guidelines: "If a staff member or volunteer and resident want to get together outside of the regular activities of Good Works, the level of accountability to Good Works is shaped by where the individuals originally met." This explanation is from Good Works' guidelines for volunteers:

> Where you as a volunteer [initially] meet the people that Good Works serves determines what kind of relationship you will have with them. If you meet them at a local restaurant, for example, Good Works will have a limited "voice" into how you conduct yourself. If you meet them through Good Works, we will expect you to listen and consider our guidance in your relationship. This means that we expect you to ask for input from your staff supervisor *prior* to exchanging contact information with or spending time with a recipient of a Good Works program outside of your volunteer setting. Recognizing the wisdom of those who served with Good Works for a long time is essential to being a volunteer.

In some cases, staff, interns, and volunteers are quite young and can be naive; occasionally they themselves send up red flags about their intentions. How to simultaneously make sure everyone is safe, and not be overcontrolling, is a challenge. So "keeping it in the light," asking permission to meet, and depending on another staff person to help the two persons grow as much as possible in discernment are all helpful practices.

Discernment and Discipleship for All

We sometimes fear that making a significant commitment to life in community is not really good for the individual, that it involves sacrifice of self in a way that is individually destructive. While substantial personal sacrifice may be necessary sometimes, that is not the aim. The aim is for all to flourish, to grow in grace and maturity. While moment to moment, there can be difficulties, life in community should be good for every person. Potential staff and interns at Good Works are encouraged to reflect on four questions as they consider whether to join Good Works. These questions are relevant more broadly to joining any community that is oriented outward or toward mission. They are helpful in discerning both potential fit and mutual flourishing.

First, *can I learn something from these people?* If the answer is no, there is not much future together. Second, *are these the kind of people who I believe can learn something from me?* Do they seem teachable? Do they expect to learn anything from the new person? Third, *is this community as concerned for my growth and development as it is about the people it reaches out to?* If not, then the situation is not sustainable. Finally, *can I experience healing too, or is it just for the "official" recipients?* Does this community recognize that I'm not completely healed, that challenges are going to trigger things in me? Is there going to be room to work with me at points of crisis, or will the community just say, "Shape up and get it done"? What kind of atmosphere will allow me to thrive and continue to receive the grace of healing?

As any organization grows and adds staff, it faces questions about how to discern fit. In the early years of Good Works, I (Keith) realized that staff members would have to be followers of Jesus with their own spiritual disciplines, recognizing that we don't have anything to offer people unless we have a private life in Christ. Initially assuming it was my role to disciple staff members as they joined, I quickly realized that it was a more mutual process. I discovered that I was receiving from them as well, and the ministry was going to be destined for fruitfulness in relationship to community. Fruit would be produced as we created an atmosphere where we constantly spur one another on, not because of someone in authority, but because of trust. While Good Works certainly has supervisory roles and there are channels of responsibility, it is the mutuality of relationships that is so powerful.

Life in community should be good for every person

This form of "horizontal discipleship" emerges when we are able to open our lives to people because we know they love us and their intentions are good. When we're willing to listen to them, they can help us become more like Jesus in a way we'll never learn through a sermon or a book. Trust and discipleship are closely connected.

Holding together freedom, initiative, discipline, and accountability is crucial for a growing community. This requires particular spiritual disciplines. "Dying to the need to be appreciated" and "keeping it in the light" were discussed in the previous section. Other important disciplines include the following:

- Patience: We depend on the guidance of the Holy Spirit to teach us how to walk in God's timing. So, we wait prayerfully, looking for opportunities to build trust with the person we seek to love, and to answer the questions they are asking. We recognize that much of the impact we have in ministry results from people trusting us.

- Perseverance: We can continue to hold out the possibility of belonging, forgiveness, and reconciled relationships because we hold on to hope. God is glorified when we persevere in showing love and, without fear, seek "to overcome evil with good." Learning to press on despite setbacks and disappointments helps us grow in maturity and fidelity.

- Erring to the side of mercy: "Mercy triumphs over judgment" (James 2:13). We pray and ask, "Lord, how can we further the work you are doing?" When we do not have clarity or unity, we make our best judgment and choose to err to the side of mercy.

- Promising: We try not to promise more than we can do and learn to assess accurately our own capacities. Mostly, we just do things, and then carefully make commitments to people, lest we disappoint them and ourselves.

- Recognizing our weaknesses: We expect that ministry will surface our unresolved issues. To help others, we need to see our own woundedness and not seek to cover up our weakness. We also try to consider how that woundedness intersects with our efforts to help and respond.

- Individual and communal worship: The good fruit of our lives emerges from our faithfulness as worshipers of God. For each individual, this involves intentional times of prayer, worship, Scripture study, and reflection. In community life, this means that we set aside regular times to nurture our relationship with God together. As we take a posture of listening, gratitude, and praise, God shows us a holy perspective on ourselves and others. We see that we are flawed but valued, as are our efforts to love others. We cannot hope to see or love our neighbor properly unless we are growing in our understanding of how God sees and loves them and us.

- Practicing sabbath and renewal: Having a rhythm that involves both building community and turning outward toward mission makes life sustainable. We guard one another's days off and vacation time; we are committed to allowing people to rest. The vision statement for Good Works' Carter Cabin explains:

> The years of ministry we have spent among very hurting and needy people have taught us about what it means to become "weary in well-doing." Out of this understanding God has shown us that we have something to offer our brothers and sisters who are tired, worn and in need of a quiet place to rest. Therefore, we have created a retreat cabin so that Christians can come to a "solitary place" (see Mark 1:35 & Luke 5:16). It is our vision to *extend* our ministry of hospitality beyond people in poverty to include servants in the kingdom who need "times of refreshing in the presence of the Lord."[3]

But What Can I Do Now?

How do we begin conversations, service, and relationships with people who are vulnerable, excluded, or struggling with poverty? What do I bring? We can start by hearing God's question to Moses as also directed to us: "What is in your hand?" (Exod. 4:2). We can begin by looking at what we have in our

3. See http://good-works.net/carter-cabin.

hands, the resources God has given us. How might we use what we already have to love our neighbors? We can talk with trusted friends who also struggle with this. But we begin by asking God how to use the resources and talents we've already been given.

As discussed in the previous chapter, in the Old Testament, God gives us three starting places: widows, fatherless children, and people who would be considered strangers—people whose social and economic circumstances are precarious and those outside the boundaries of our normal social interactions. We can

*God gives us three
starting places: widows,
fatherless children,
and ... strangers*

start by thinking about the relationships and social networks that we already have. Is there someone who lives nearby whom we could pray for, or a person we might begin a conversation with—a conversation that could open into the next level of friendship? If we don't know of anyone in these circumstances, we should ask ourselves whether we are too insulated or whether we might be blind to the people around us.

Perhaps before any of these steps toward engagement, some of us might need to admit or confess that we aren't sure we want a relationship with any of "those people." Our viewpoints have often been shaped by thinking and concerns separate from Christ's love. James 1:27 reminds us to look after orphans and widows and keep ourselves from being polluted by the world. Could the danger of being polluted by the world include embracing wrong attitudes toward those who are poor or vulnerable? We all have fears and apprehensions. Facing our fears, naming them, and talking with another person about them help us bring them into the light and allow us to move forward toward first steps in connecting with people.

Often, it helps to find a friend who is willing to walk with us on this journey; Jesus sent his disciples out in pairs. Volunteering together in a local ministry or service organization can expose us to needs and to people in our own community whom we might not encounter in our regular patterns of life.

Finally, we can recognize that this takes time and often happens at the edges or margins of our daily tasks. If everything about our lives is tightly scheduled, we will have little time to make room for others or to respond spontaneously to persons or opportunities to connect. We can pray that the Lord will help us learn to set aside time and space so that we can build a platform for generosity.

Henri Nouwen's description of his own growth in this area captures much of the journey toward friendship:

> More and more, the desire grows in me simply to walk around, greet people, enter their homes, sit on their doorsteps, play ball . . . and be known as someone who wants to live with them. It is a privilege to have the time . . . to practice this simple ministry of presence. Still, it is not as simple as it seems. My own desire to be useful, to do something significant, or to be part of some impressive project is so strong that soon my time is taken up by meetings, conferences, study groups, and workshops that prevent me from walking the streets. It is difficult not to have plans, not to organize people around an urgent cause, and not to feel that you are working directly for social progress.
>
> But I wonder more and more if the first thing shouldn't be to know people by name, to eat and drink with them, to listen to their stories and tell your own, and to let them know with words, handshakes, and hugs that you do not simply like them, but truly love them.[4]

4. Henri J. M. Nouwen, *Gracias! A Latin American Journal* (Maryknoll, NY: Orbis Books, 1993), 147-48.

"Doing for" is the approach that most middle-class Americans choose when attempting to connect with people who are poor or vulnerable. Then "getting it done" or being efficient and having measurable results are crucial. We tend to frame up service in a way that says, "I'm in control, and I determine what I'm going to do for you, and I get it done." "Doing with" is a more vulnerable stance, when I'm no longer in control. "Being with" is an expression of the familiarity and grace of friendship that is mutual. It is also a recognition that some people need the gift of presence as much as—if not more than—the things we can do for them.

Congregations sometimes look for practical suggestions for where to start when we want to do ministry with people struggling with poverty. One possibility is to take a year to find out what is already being done in the community and to help out with that. It means joining in someone else's mission—not if it violates conscience, but otherwise, we can help out with what's already going on. We could then begin a regular dialogue in the church, once or twice a month, and talk about what is happening, what we are learning, and where we see gaps. At the end of the year, the congregation will have a better sense of where it might step in. Such an approach provides the time necessary to discern this and to start building trust with people in the neighborhood.

How Do We Know Whether We Have Succeeded?

What is success in ministry or in friendship? Can it be measured? Or is success the wrong category? Maybe it's about faithfulness? I (Keith) want to be able to say to the Lord, "I was faithful with the ones you gave me."[5] If we begin with

5. See John 17.

being faithful to walk in the light, to do what we believe the Lord has given us to do, we will always achieve some measure of success.

But wrestling with our desire for people to experience salvation and full restoration through Jesus, we ask ourselves the question that others also pose: "How much success are you having?" At Good Works, two answers exist in tension with each other but might be better under- *How much success are* stood as on a "continuum of success." On one *you having?* end of this continuum is a type of achievement that has no immediate visible results in the lives of others but is an expression of our faithfulness. Mother Teresa said it well: "God has not called me to be successful, he has called me to be faithful." Here, we realize that true success understood simply as pleasing God is found whenever we are obedient and willing to walk in the instruction that God has already shown us. Surprisingly, the Lord often glues together our small acts of faithfulness and gives them back to us in the form of deeper faith. With faith, we are able to trust God more fully and have confidence that our labor is producing long-lasting fruit, even if it isn't recognizable in the moment.

On the other end of the continuum, we realize that when we are faithful, our lives and efforts should produce good fruit. The fruit of our lives will be evident in healing for others, in their reconciled relationships, and in their integration within the body of Christ—embraced and participating as fully functioning members of a local Christian community or church congregation.

In the regular efforts of helping at Good Works, if we embrace the notion of striving for success, is it appropriate and "successful" to have offered someone something to eat? Of course it is! To have provided a bed? Well, yes! And that in itself has value, regardless of whether anything else follows. Those provisions are not simply a means to another end; they are a valuable expression of the love of God and stand on their own. If nothing ever happens after that and if we never see them again, it is still a good thing and an act of worship to have given food and shelter. But it isn't full success. Perhaps we get to hear their story and share our testimony. Is that success? Well, yes, but not really. Then maybe a relationship develops and trust is established and they want to come to church with us. Is that success? Of course, and yet, still not fully. Then they give their lives to Christ and they become his followers. Is that success? Yes, but it is still not the end goal. The end goal is when they become participating members of a local community of believers where they can receive nurture, care, and accountability, and where they can identify and use the gifts that God has given them. When they are in that place, then and only then have we truly achieved success.

With this understanding of success, fruitfulness for Good Works is deeply reliant on the willing participation of people in local congregations. When local believers make themselves available for genuine relationships with people struggling with poverty, they each can share their gifts, can be embraced into fellowship with the body of Christ, and can be restored to hope, healing, and wholeness.

Conclusion

A community of friends is beautiful and challenging, filled with possibilities and risks, joys and disappointments. Within it, we can grow and flourish, as we move more deeply into faithful discipleship. Every community—even those characterized by deep life-giving friendships—requires some form of leadership, the subject of the next chapter.

Prayer

Let our choice of friends—our social lives—be pleasing to you,
Lord. May the life of Jesus be manifest in and through us.
Give us your heart so that we can make room for others who
long for a place to belong, to contribute, to grow. Let our
lives and our communities be transformed into your likeness
by the people we welcome.
Amen.

Questions for Reflection and Discussion

1. How is your church a safe place for people who are poor, without homes, or struggling with addiction? What could you build on to strengthen the good that is already happening?

2. Are there lifestyle choices you could make that would make it easier to form relationships with people different from yourself in terms of socioeconomic status, race, ethnicity, etc.?

3. Do you see yourself as insulated or engaged? Are people in your life struggling with poverty or exclusion? Where are those relationships on the continuum of associating—serving—loving—knowing? Share about one of those relationships.

4. Which spiritual disciplines have been most helpful to you in your ministries of outreach and witness? Which ones have you done individually and which have you engaged in corporately? What could you add after reading this chapter?

5. How do you struggle with tensions between "getting it done" and building relationships?

6. How do you navigate the tension between success and faithfulness, or do you see a tension there?

7. Three questions are key in shaping a life-giving environment. Who are the poor in your context, what is the gospel
   (do we all understand it similarly), and how do we bring it
   (are our methods immersed in love)? These are questions
   every congregation can ask. How would you respond?
8. In what ways might poverty, or experience with some forms
   of poverty, bring you closer to God and to the kingdom?
9. What would it look like for you and a small group to take a
   year and volunteer in your community and reflect together
   to identify gaps in ministry that you could help address?

FIVE

Leadership in Community

Looking back over my journey into leadership, I (Keith) often say that God gave me the gift of naivete; had I known then what I know now, I never would have started a shelter for people without homes in the basement of my own house. But God used my not knowing to get me to do something I would never have done if I'd known what I was doing. It's a mystery of faith that was true for Abraham and Moses as well. God doesn't tell us the whole story but instead says, "Trust me," and confirms the one essential ingredient that we need for the journey—his presence.

The encounter between God and Moses in Exodus 3–4 continues to challenge me. As Moses turns away from the burning bush, God says to him, "remove the sandals from your feet." And I wonder in response, "Okay, is there something I should be removing to hear God's voice?" Next, the Lord says, "I have observed the misery of my people. . . . I have heard their cry. . . . I know their suf- *The presence of God is the primary ingredient we need for the mission of God* ferings. . . ." And I ask myself, "Do I see the sufferings of people? Am I concerned about the misery of people who are vulnerable or oppressed? Am I hearing them cry out?"

Then God says, "So come, I will send you. . . ." You can feel the chills going through Moses as he wonders, "You talkin' to me?" And the first thing out of Moses's mouth in response is, "Who am I?" It seems like one of the big questions we will wrestle with when God calls us to a place of ministry. It's like a rite of passage. But God's answer to Moses's question isn't "Well, let's talk about you and your capacities." It's "I will be with you." Whoa. That doesn't answer the question Moses asked, but it is the answer Moses needed. The presence of God is the primary ingredient we need for the mission of God.

Then Moses asks another question, which is basically, "Who are you? What am I going to tell people who ask?" Here the knowing—the answer—is in the going. God tells him, "I am who I am. . . . Go. . . ." The answer comes in the nitty gritty messiness of going. And so "who are you" questions are our intersections with God's purposes.

Then Moses asks, "But suppose they do not believe me or listen to me . . . ?" If we are not coming to this question, we probably aren't in the mission. Every one of us will wonder at some point, "We put this thing together, but what if folks don't show up, what if they don't come?" This is the right question to be asking; it is another rite of passage. And the Lord answers Moses with another question: "What is that in your hand?" Huh? What's that got to do with it? For Moses, it's a staff, and God tells him to throw it down. For me it was a house. I had a house, and God said, "Release it. Release that house to me, and I will turn it into something far beyond your wildest dreams."

The next response of Moses is an act of resistance; he tells God that he can't do it. We all come to this point in our journey. We're going to come to the end of our ability, and the sooner the better. Whether it is our talents, skills, credentials, or experience, each of us will come to a place where we say, "I can't. I quit. There's no way." And God gives an abrupt, in-your-face answer. To Moses, who said he couldn't speak, God asks, "Who gives speech . . . ?" God promises Moses, "I will be with your mouth and teach you what you are to speak." The Lord will use our weaknesses in a way that God does not work in our strengths.

Then Moses actually says to God, "Please send someone else." We should be warned by that response, because following it we read that the anger of the Lord burned against Moses. It is not a response the Lord wants to hear from us. Isaiah's response to God's call (Isa. 6:8) is far better: "Here am I. Send me!" The questions and answers we encounter in this story really capture the journey we go through in fulfilling the mission of God.[1]

There are countless books and articles on leadership today and many have important insights. Leadership is difficult, and leading in a way that takes the practices of community seriously is particularly challenging. At the core of leadership-in-community, there are holy tensions that are not resolvable by having victory over one tension or even by holding the tensions in balance.[2] These tensions are necessary, even good, and important to maintain. They are not at odds with each other, but they do pull in different directions and contribute to the challenges of leadership.

Three central insights have emerged from four decades of leadership: (1) leadership is lonely; (2) ministry is fragile; and (3) fruit—the kind that will remain—takes years to produce. Within these three insights are very significant tensions. Despite the fact that no community can manage all the tensions well all the time, living with the tensions is part of the life-giving nature of ministry in community.

1. All biblical quotations in this account of Moses's encounter with God are taken from the New Revised Standard Version of the Bible.

2. One definition of *holy* is "set apart for the purposes of God." In a sense, maintaining these tensions allows the purposes of God to go forward.

Leadership Is Lonely

Every community needs some kind of leadership, but often the experience of leadership in community is lonely. How can that be? How can a person deeply rooted in community feel lonely? Here are some of the tensions:

Assessing Individual Situations and Institutional Needs

An important commitment for leadership-in-community is to help shape new leaders and encourage them in their acts of faith. While we would not want to usurp the authority and initiative of the very leaders we have helped raise up, we still need to be able to speak into the decisions they are making, especially when those decisions have implications for the sustainability of the organization or community. Experienced leaders are continually assessing and observing the dynamics of the group and the individuals within it while, at the same time, being part of the group. Whatever his or her specific job description, part of the leader's role is to look for ways the community—as a community—can experience the fullness of life together while at the same time attending to individual flourishing and growth.

Wisdom in these dynamics is crucial. Leaders need foresight to think through an individual situation in relation to the well-being of the larger group in order to avoid undermining the group or the individual. Sometimes individuals will say, "Lord, I'll do anything," but it is not really in their capacity to do certain things, and it will impact the group negatively if they try and fail. In other cases, it is crucial to give people the freedom to succeed or fail at risky endeavors. Discerning this within community can be challenging and lonely. People need to know that they are valued and trusted so that they can both take risks and receive correction or help.

Part of the challenge for leaders is being willing to entrust work to others while still carrying final responsibility for the process and the outcome. We are sometimes hesitant to delegate work because if it is not done well, we fear it will reflect badly on us as leaders or badly on the organization. Even with a strong commitment to helping people grow and mature, sometimes the process of delegation is quite risky. On the other hand, this is an excellent way to deepen discipleship and to encourage the development of initiative and responsibility. One of the challenges for leaders is to learn to assess the strengths and weaknesses in individuals and communities and to sort out how they as leaders can stand in the gap.

Leaders must constantly make decisions, not necessarily alone, but the process can be lonely and subject at times to misunderstanding. We must attend to the moment, the everydayness of messy relationships and unexpected opportunities, while maintaining a vision for the future. There is a complicated dynamic of being part of a community and also being one of its observers or assessors.

Dealing with Failure

Good leaders are in touch with their weaknesses and admit their need for help from God and other people. I (Keith) often think that Good Works is more a testimony to my weaknesses than to my strengths. Wise leaders give permission to others—in the right context—to help them grow in their areas of weakness. Without attending to those weaknesses, it is very easy to lead the community astray, but again there are risks with this level of vulnerability.

Within community, leaders need to be able to absorb difficulty, complaint, and criticism while having a robust theology of forgiveness. Wise leaders struggle to hold together delicate relationships among people who are at various levels of maturity.

It is important to recognize that we can learn much through failure, and making friends with failure allows us to learn things we couldn't learn through success. However, while we might be happy to talk about allowing ourselves and others the freedom to fail, when we fail on other people, it is a problem. So leaders have to measure and anticipate consequences even as they value and encourage freedom and initiative.

Humility and Teachableness

Good leaders are often good teachers, but they must cultivate a simultaneous identity as learners. Such leaders learn through patience, humility, and love. Humility is particularly important in trying to learn from our own mistakes and from the mistakes of others, but it is also important as we learn from rebukes and corrections from within and outside the community. We pray, "Help me to hear you in this, Lord. Is this accurate information that I need to ponder, or is this coming from someone who is embittered, and I need to simply find a way to absorb it?" Not all criticism and rebuke are constructive or warranted, and this requires discernment as leaders who embody humility also open themselves to criticism. Trusted friends can help us sort out some of these challenges.

Being above Reproach and Approachable

To have the credibility necessary for leading a community, a person's integrity is essential. Leaders lead best by example, and leadership requires a level of self-discipline that recognizes that any significant gap between one's teaching and practices undoes both authority and credibility.

Self-revelation and authenticity are crucial, but good leaders must also sometimes remove themselves from things others can do (Rom. 14:13). Leaders wrestle in distinct ways with the challenge of Jesus to be in the world but not of it, and it is important to remember the principle that "to whom much is given, much shall be required" (John 17:15–16; Luke 12:48). *Good leadership is good in public and in private* Good leadership is good in public and in private. In a sense, leaders in community are "on" all the time.

However, commitments to truthfulness and integrity do not always protect leaders and organizations from complaints or false accusations. For a leader, an accusation about his or her leadership and integrity can have a major impact on the ministry—regardless of whether it is true. More is at stake than personal feelings or reputation; the well-being of the entire organization can be at risk.

These are very complicated situations, and when a staff member or volunteer brings a complaint against an individual leader, it can be helpful to handle it with a team—brought into the discussion from the beginning. Especially when the accusation or complaint is against the main leader, a senior staff or board member should be brought in very early in the process. It is crucial for communities and ministries to have protocols in place to deal quickly but carefully with moral failures in leaders.

Truthfulness

Good leaders cultivate the courage to speak the truth in love, even when it is not to their personal benefit. Living a truthful life requires kindness, grace, and discernment. Because of their friendships across the spectrum of spiritual and moral matu-

rity, leaders seek to be faithful and truthful, while also cultivating wisdom about appropriate levels of self-disclosure or
transparency.

Character and Adversity

The wisdom Paul offered to Timothy in appointing leaders re-
mains relevant today. A strong emphasis on character is evident
in the instructions to let potential leaders "first be tested" and
then let them serve if they are above reproach (1 Tim. 3:10). But
it is difficult to know the character of a person until we see how
he or she deals with difficult people and adversity. In a sense,
adversity is a friend, and how a person reacts to it will reveal his
or her level of integrity and capacity for responsibility. While a
person may occasionally "fail" the test, if she or he is teachable
and willing to grow in maturity and responsibility, the experience can yield good fruit.

Sacrifice

For Christian leaders, sacrifice is not an occasional act, it is a way
of life. This sacrifice is often greater than what is or can be asked
of most staff members or volunteers. Some level of sacrifice is
basic to all leadership, and this becomes more complicated in a
place like Good Works where staff members view themselves
both as in ministry and as employees. An employment paradigm relating to policies, job descriptions, contracts, hours, and
compensation is protective and necessary. At the same time, it is
insufficient for explaining what it means to be on staff, because
there are other important commitments at work. Expectations
of a nine-to-five job bump up against the commitment to "do life
together" when the emphasis is on building relationships and

strengthening discipleship. Sacrifices are often necessary for everyone, but for committed Christian leaders, sacrifice is not an occasional, difficult choice; it becomes a lifestyle.

Willing sacrifices by leaders impart moral authority and credibility within the community. Leaders sometimes sacrifice their own experiences of community for the sake of the community they are leading. Perhaps they are gone for extended periods, or maintain demanding travel schedules and experience loneliness, even as they work on behalf of the community. Managing time wisely while being available and approachable is a constant challenge.

Sometimes sacrifice comes in the form of a wilderness experience, which seems like another rite of passage for fruitfulness in ministry. Almost every leader endures these periods, and they are often very lonely. Through the experiences, however, God is able to develop new forms of maturity, insight, obedience, and tenderness in the leader.

Jesus is our example for a time in the wilderness as a prelude to ministry and for sacrifice at the end of his earthly ministry. Both were times of loneliness despite a community of friends. It is part of leadership-in-community—to be at the center and to be lonely.

Ministry Is Fragile

Ministry in community is fragile; a loss of integrity on the part of the leader can blow the organization apart. But separate from such failures, community life involves relationships among broken people, and while a community depends on trust, trust is also easily undermined by the woundedness of the very people we depend on. Even so, trust within community can develop a certain sturdiness that allows those involved to navigate the difficulties and withstand the failures. Here are some of the other challenges:

Building Trust and Using Power

The capacity to lead a community comes from the relationships a leader forms and from the credibility and trustworthiness that flow from the leader's integrity. But trust is easily undermined by deceit, misuse of power, and failures in accountability. In fact, deceit will destroy any hope leaders might have that they will be doing what God has called them to do. Practicing honesty with oneself is prior even to honesty with others.

Leadership involves a capacity to influence people, and influence involves how we use power. Using power for good requires commitment, and accountability to both God and persons in our community—both vertical and horizontal responsibility. Whether it is expressed overtly or with great subtlety, our own need for power and the dangers of misusing power are constant threats in ministry. Anchored in the fear of God and the love and accountability of a community, however, leaders can cultivate discernment that allows us to recognize our own desire for power and control. The impulse to manipulate others through the power we have is particularly dangerous, especially if we have convinced ourselves that the goal is so important that manipulation is warranted.

The impulse to manipulate others through the power we have is particularly dangerous

Leaders who found organizations or ministries frequently begin as "one-person shows." These founders are often mavericks who are skilled at getting things done. As the ministry expands, it is important to learn discernment about where to invite others into decision-making and where to continue to make decisions on one's own. This is a holy tension in community, because, if you put everything out for everyone to decide and try for consensus on every detail, people quickly become frustrated. And yet, in many cases, it is crucial to include others in the decisions to develop a shared vision and to encourage a sense of ownership.

A challenge that leaders often face in community is consistency—distinguishing between precedent and exception. When people work in close proximity to one another, there are many reasons for comparison. "But you did it for him, so why can't you do it for me?" kinds of responses can be very complicated in community. There should be significant reasons for making exceptions in resources or freedoms available to staff members because—without good reasons—the decision becomes a precedent that others then expect to be available to all. This involves the foresight and discernment of experienced leaders to know when an individual needs an exception to be made, and when it will lead to serious difficulties later.

Woundedness and Suffering

Within the community, it is important to acknowledge that all of us need healing and that we will take time to help one another toward wholeness. Of course, some healing will come from outside the community, but without the work and support of the community to which we're connected on a daily basis, it is hard to address individual woundedness. Despite the challenges this involves, community is not sustainable without such work.

Our woundedness, sometimes carried over many years, is something God can use, regardless of when we experience complete or full healing. But in working with staff and volunteers, leaders must discern the level of woundedness in proportion to the level of responsibility given. Wounds can come as a result of many things, including sin and having been sinned against. Sometimes people use a great deal of energy to hide these wounds, but even the hidden ones impact how people function in community.

Especially when working with people who are vulnerable and who have been violated or exploited, we can encounter heartbreaking suffering. As we come alongside them in their suffering or when we experience it ourselves, we learn firsthand that there is suffering we do not understand and did not cause, and there is suffering that occurs because the choices we've made have consequences. Often multiple factors are present. But, in any case, God is willing to meet us and can give us purpose in the suffering. While we may not understand this, we can trust that God's presence will be with us. When communities choose to walk alongside members who are suffering, it can be very difficult but also can strengthen the community and its members. Prolonged suffering, however, can also reveal the cracks, fissures, and fragility in community.

The Power and Dangers of Affirmation

Leaders can have enormous influence through affirmation. To be true affirmation, however, it should be the result of close attention to who the individuals are, what they've been through, and what is operating behind the scenes. Leaders can work to find what motivates and affirms a person, and they can be more pastoral and less directive when they can affirm what is good.

For example, at the weekly staff gatherings at Good Works, the time begins with prayer and then moves to affirmations—a ritual of the community. Much is very genuine, spontaneous affirmation that is both moving and beautiful. Sometimes it is directed toward an individual on the staff. Other times, it might be directed toward someone who is visiting but is also known by some in the community. Those who offer the affirmations identify very particular things they have noticed about the individual and what the community wants to celebrate about him or her. This practice has been so appreciated by staff at Good Works that when they leave, they often take the practice to the next place they work.

Of course, affirmation can also be misused—when it is flattery or manipulation. It has a temporary impact, though the dishonesty becomes apparent quite quickly in community, so that the danger of misuse is reduced when affirmations are offered in group settings. An overemphasis on encouragement and affirmation can also make it hard to offer rebuke or even constructive criticism within community. As Christian leaders it is important to help people learn to distinguish between using good judgment and being judgmental. Fears of "judgmentalism" or fracturing trust by identifying problems and making hard decisions can paralyze an organization and its staff and undermine its capacity to make important moral distinctions and claims.

If a person leads an organization, does a lot of public speaking, or writes books, it is possible to find oneself with a dedicated fan club. It is easy to be taken in by the attention and adulation, and it is dangerous. Soon we want more, and sometimes we are willing to manipulate others to get it. We all need affirmation and encouragement. Truthful, uncoerced times of gratitude and affirmation allow God's encouragement to be spoken and heard as it comes through the words and appreciation of other people. A culture of affirmation enables us to hear the affirmation of God.

Slow Growing Fruit

Discipleship requires patient cultivation of persons toward growth and wholeness. This involves increasing trust, strengthening character, and encouraging yieldedness to God. Even in an organization with staff positions and responsibilities to others, these factors are more important than qualifications, accumulation of knowledge, or expertise.

The one thing I (Keith) most want to model—and what I look for in other people—is not credentials; it is yieldedness to Christ—evident in a willingness to open our lives to allow God to work in us and through us. Sometimes we want God to work through us but not in us. That would be unsustainable in the Good Works community. If staff members are struggling with something, we want to surround them as part of a support system that allows for the work of God in them. We pray for wisdom, so that whatever the issue, we can help it become a contributor to their development as disciples and coworkers.

In fostering discipleship and in assessing growth in staff members, it is especially important to be attentive to what happens behind the scenes. As noted earlier, one definition of integrity is what people are doing when they think no one is looking and no one will find out. But I (Keith) am looking. I'm looking to promote people, not dismantle them. I'm asking myself, how can I accentuate a strength here and help move the person to the next level? Maturity and integrity are so often apparent in the hidden responses, in how the person deals with problems and failures. When something goes wrong, is the person defensive or willing to take responsibility? Does he or she ask for forgiveness? I put the capacity to give and receive forgiveness at the center of Christian maturity.

Identifying people who should be promoted to leadership and who can be given more responsibility and power in other people's lives involves assessing their maturity and trustworthiness in little things. Leaders can create environments where testing comes early. As integrity is demonstrated, individuals can be given more responsibility. This takes time, and a good leader often needs to slow down the process.

A helpful but uncommon sequence for promotion is that before individuals are given a title or position, they are given some power and then observed to see how they respond; we want to give power to those who pass integrity tests. While it is possible to disciple people who are not fully trustworthy, we cannot give them responsibility over others. At

While it is possible to disciple people who are not fully trustworthy, we cannot give them responsibility over others

Good Works, persons have occasionally been promoted to leadership who are significantly younger than some of their coworkers, but based on their character, their "testedness," and their ability to handle delicate things, it has been appropriate.

Because of a willingness to move slowly and to cultivate discipleship, some folks at Good Works who started as recipients of help have moved to being participants and volunteers, and from volunteers to staff members and leadership roles. This rarely happens quickly, but the resulting blessings are significant, both in terms of personal transformation and also in benefit to the group, which is strengthened by their wisdom, insight, and credibility.

A community that welcomes individuals at various levels of maturity and discipleship and encourages close and truthful relationships across differences will encounter significant tensions and challenges. Relationships can be delicate and complicated, but these relationships, when built slowly over time, also give glimpses of God's grace and patience at work.

We now turn to two additional challenges or tensions that we have encountered in cultivating long-term fruitfulness.

Encouraging Accountability and Autonomy

When a ministry is highly relational and based in a particular community, much of the leadership can and probably should be grown from within the organization. While there are risks that an organization can become ingrown, it is crucial to have leaders who know the culture, share the vision, and have demonstrated commitment to the community over time.

Shaping people toward leadership roles is a slow and sometimes cumbersome process. It involves developing a deeper and deeper sense of accountability while also encouraging increasing levels of autonomy. Accountability is evident as a person becomes clearer about lines of authority and when those can or should be crossed. It is also evident in how a person relates both to the community and to the supervisory structures. Maturity is demonstrated when a person has moved beyond an attitude such as "I'm sorry—that you caught me" and toward "I need to tell you something you have no idea about. I need to tell you this, and I apologize." With a growth in accountability and a deep-rooted sense of responsibility to the community, persons then have a clearer sense of authority and ownership, and when they should ask permission and when to make decisions on their own. This kind of liberty holds authority, ownership, and accountability in a holy tension and opens up new ways for persons to contribute to the community.

For the main leaders of a ministry, accountability is particularly important. They are accountable not only to a board of directors but also to the whole community. Leaders are often at risk when they choose "yes" people for their boards and staff, people who are easily impressed or quickly defer to them. King David and countless leaders after him ran into trouble because they had power without accountability, thinking they could do as they pleased and then cover up their sins—that is, until someone like the prophet Nathan came along (2 Sam. 12:1–15).

The goal of accountability is holiness, and faithful leaders do not wait to form accountable relationships; they initiate them. To truly bear fruit, it is important to create a climate where people sense permission or freedom to admonish their leaders without fearing repercussions. This requires a significant level of trust within the community and usually requires time to develop. Staff members learn whether it is safe to confront, and whether senior leaders will invite and receive admonition. While this can also involve a level of risk as the critic may take advantage at the point the leader has made himself or herself vulnerable, openness to criticism and correction is central to good leadership.

Addressing Innovation, Drift, and Sustainability

Part of what makes Good Works a vibrant ministry is the way it has combined innovation and faithfulness over the years. Innovation depends on creative leaders who have cultivated a yielded spirit and an empowered staff. For example, Good Works encountered difficulty with expanding the Timothy House property to address the growing need for providing shelter for people without homes. My wife, Darlene, and I (Keith) eventually decided to purchase a house in the immediate neighborhood and moved there. We opened a section of our new home to guests who needed a place when the Timothy House was full. This was within city regulations and worked within the regular Good Works processes to screen prospective guests. It was not a return to the early days when Good Works was located in our basement, but it was not completely different either. This new model involves the Good Works staff while allowing us to be a "host" family. It also provides other concerned persons with a model for helping that could operate at a personal and sustainable level.

Another early innovation at Good Works put us ahead of the trend in working with volunteers who do not identify themselves as Christians. Recognizing that participating in good works is important in spiritual and moral formation and fulfills a human hunger to serve others, Good Works has found their involvement to be a blessing in several ways. Volunteers from all walks of life, alongside Christians, serve people in need and are changed by the experience. In the context of a non-profit Christian ministry, their help is needed and valued.

Encouraging staff members to dream dreams and initiate projects are other expressions of innovation. Over the years, Good Works has learned that when such projects involve significant investment, it is important that the staff member has demonstrated a commitment to the Good Works community, the region, and its people. Otherwise, innovation is too temporary and disruptive. But if the individuals will stay because they love the people and the community, then there are real possibilities.

Innovation also means recognizing that people's roles can change within an organization. Leaders can provide structures in which staff members can experiment with and take on new roles. But leaders and the founders themselves sometimes need to find new roles. Over the years, I (Keith) have changed from a founder/director to a sustainer/director. The skills and approach necessary to lead well after forty years are quite different from those it took to get things started, and had the innovations not occurred, the organization would probably not have survived.

When Good Works first began, I was running an organization 24/7 out of my home. When the ministry moved to a separate location, I was still on call. These days, things have to escalate significantly for me to intervene, though I will sometimes call in and ask what is going on. But I won't interfere to the point of usurping anyone's role in the organization. If the person on call wants to consult with me, I'm happy to do that, but in the case of a volunteer's question, I would direct him or her to the on-call person. Usurping the authority of another person sends a terrible message.

In the early days of Good Works, I did form "bad habits" by being "on" all the time. It was very fulfilling—to be needed (and I was needed)—but I'm not needed in that way anymore. Adjusting to such a change in role is often challenging for leaders and founders. And, in fact, it requires a retooling of leadership skills to stay with an organization over decades. It also requires key people to help a leader make such changes—people on the staff or the board of directors as well as friends from outside the organization.

A passage in chapter 2 of Mark's Gospel has given me insight into innovation-in-community. Four men wanted to bring their paralyzed friend to Jesus but were not able to get through the crowd that had gathered around the house Jesus was in. One of them must have had the bold idea to lower their friend through the roof of the house and persuaded the other three to go along. For me this has been an allegory for my own life. I too want to carry my friends to a place where they can hear and experience Jesus saying, "Which is easier: to say, . . . 'your sins are forgiven' or to say, 'get up . . . and walk?'" I too am continually searching for spontaneous and organizational ways to lead people to this place, but I also realize that I cannot lead people to these places by myself. Much of my life has been spent figuring out ways to persuade my friends to walk with me as I and they carry others to the place where all of us can experience Jesus's healing. I have had to learn the "art" of inviting people who share my passion to take the risks of innovation, and many times, we have had to use unconventional ways (like going through a roof) to help people experience the personal and transformational touch that Jesus alone provides.

Discerning the difference between innovation and "drift," however, is a regular challenge, especially as an organization matures. Drift is shorthand for what happens when an organization gradually moves away from its original mission and deepest commitments. Innovation is a process by which an organization makes adjustments to address changes in context, leadership, needs, or resources, while keeping in line with its primary mission and commitments.

To resist drift and remain sustainable, Good Works celebrates its history and focuses on its core commitments and mission. Over the decades, the community has been very wary of allowing financial pressures to drive decisions and has been willing to turn down money if the gift was not going to further the mission. Funding does not have the final word. Careful attention to staff development and growth, and to how key people join the community, has also helped Good Works resist drift.

Because of concerns about sustainability, the risk of being drawn away from one's primary vision or mission is always significant. In ministries like Good Works, there are additional pressures. There is a risk that the Great Commandment will be flipped, and we imagine that we should love our neighbors with all our heart, soul, mind, and strength and God as ourselves. Such a move turns people in need into idols and quickly relinquishes the emphasis on spiritual growth and worshiping God. For Good Works, what keeps a Christian ministry "Christian" is that those in leadership have a vibrant faith and those on the front lines of mission have a personal relationship with Christ. That allows Good Works to welcome people who don't identify as Christians to serve alongside as volunteers with less concern about drifting away from the original vision and values.

Discerning the difference between innovation and "drift" . . . is a regular challenge

Many people wonder and worry about sustainability as an organization ages. They often associate sustainability with financing the organization, but sustainability is also about innovation and about how people continue to find a life-giving place in the ministry. Staff members have different needs based on their individual circumstances, family situations, and stages in life. So it involves learning what actually makes people want to carry on with a sense of devotion and loyalty, and how they can stay in the organization even when they don't want to continue in their particular job. Are there ways to expand the vision of the organization so people can change roles? Once staff members have made and kept a commitment to the organization for some time, how can we listen to their passions and encourage their vision rather than only invite them to join our vision?

Sustainability also means encouraging life-giving rhythms for the staff and organization. While in some settings there is a tendency to use staff members until they are used up, that does not honor those persons, nor does it represent a responsible understanding of fidelity or service. Christian organizations should be models of how staff members are cared for well and protected from misuse or exploitation, even as the group pursues worthy and demanding goals.

Potential leaders, especially when there has been a single founder and director, can be developed and tested when that founder is deliberately absent for a time. Obviously, this involves risk, but if the organization is strong enough to function well in the absence of the primary leader, his or her absence can be used as a significant mechanism for growing new leaders. At Good Works, I (Keith) have done this for several decades, leaving for three months every couple of years. My being fully absent allows—even requires—others to grow into new roles.

Longevity, Finishing Well, and Succession

Longevity

Forty years is a long time to do anything. But to stay rooted in a single community with a particular calling and vision is unusual and yields important insights about the blessings and risks of longevity. Contributing factors to longevity include integrity, self-discipline, and joy. Integrity is a leader's most important asset, and to lead a community over a long period, leaders learn to guard it. Self-discipline keeps leaders from foolish mistakes and dangerous self-indulgence. And joy in the journey makes sacrificial ministry sustainable.

Joy within community is the invisible force that keeps me (Keith) going. I say this when we bring people into the community: over time, 60 percent of this has got to be good, fun, enjoyable. If not, it's not sustainable. Forty percent is going to be hard, no question about it. We don't need to be specific about percentages, but we have to cultivate a community that is celebratory, loves one another, and enjoys the work we're doing.

Integrity is a leader's most important asset

The fidelity or trustworthiness of an organization affects the way both insiders and outsiders perceive the ministry. Within the organization, long-term leadership often fosters stability, and that same longevity contributes to credibility with those outside the organization. Years of experience can prevent common pitfalls within the ministry and can inspire others to action and faithfulness.

Longevity also affects how staff concerns are handled. Based on Jesus's pattern with his disciples and our experience over the years, we have learned that most things should be done in pairs and not alone. Community members err to the side of consultation and try to develop, remember, and use the policies that have been created to guide the group. Newer staff members are expected to learn from the more experienced staff members. Longevity has led to a deeper concern about the moral purity and right relationships of every staff person.

Long-term staff members provide the community with confirmation, wisdom, and encouragement. Newcomers and those who have been with the ministry for a while bring questions that help the community evaluate what is being done. While there is always a temptation to be defensive when questions are raised, remaining both teachable and faithful allows folks to ask, "Lord, what are you trying to teach us in this mix of experience?"

There is also a sense of clarity and patience that comes with longevity; an organization can learn to wait on God. Longevity helps a community avoid the difficulties that come with making rushed decisions. Many problems result if attention is focused on the wrong things or when people are unwilling to wait. An experienced leader is able to point out what others are not noticing and is able to head off anxiety by warning staff members of a challenge that might be emerging.

Over time, the Good Works community has also learned how to hold on to its original vision while encouraging staff to contribute to the vision for the organization. Resources and time are allocated for staff-inspired innovations, such as an emphasis on spiritual-formation retreats and expanding the ministry in agriculture, among many others.

Long-term ministry can also help establish a community's or a person's place in the larger community. I (Keith) feel respected in the city. Community leaders recognize and value our work. I know most of them. Good Works is a witness by our actions, and staff members are regularly invited to sit in on meetings and task forces within the larger community. Longevity also affects our capacity to recruit volunteers. When an organization is perceived as responsible, safe, and innovative, schools are more likely to send volunteers and interns and to trust it to provide a valuable mentoring experience.

Also, when Good Works addresses a matter in public, we have a voice, though we are careful in our public posture to take positions on the issues with which we are most directly involved. When we took a strong and costly stand against a newly implemented state government policy that would seriously intrude into the privacy of a person who is experiencing homelessness, respect for our organization increased.

Finishing Well

For any leader, finishing well comes from a pattern of living well; over the years, it is shaped by the choices we make and the changes we navigate. But it is important that the community also helps its leaders finish well. I (Keith) pray daily for God to help me finish well. Money, sex, and power are issues many leaders contend with. On our journey with Jesus, we need to guard our walk with these and other temptations in view. We need to include personal disciplines that prepare us for what we know we will encounter—betrayal and our own sin. Our lives should be a preparation for finishing well. I pray regularly, "Please don't let me do anything that would rob me of my place in the kingdom of God."

Of course, finishing well is more than avoiding moral failure. Finishing well is also about producing good fruit. It requires coming to grips with one's own finiteness and need for rest and renewal, even or especially in the midst of the pressures of ministry. Finishing well also means taking responsibility to help the organization handle one's departure well.

Succession

One way to think about staff and volunteer formation and development is to see it as a part of fulfilling the Great Commission. More than forming better coworkers or more effective colleagues, we can participate in shaping more mature disciples of Jesus.[3]

Shaping leadership for succession also comes as long-term staff members have opportunities to invest in short-term vol-

---

3. For me (Keith), Robert Coleman's *The Master Plan of Evangelism* has been very helpful, because of the framework Coleman provides of demonstration, reproduction, supervision, delegation, and impartation as part of discipleship and leadership development.

unteers and interns. The experience is often as formative for the staff person as for the intern or volunteer. In addition, some of the short-term coworkers become the long-term staff members. Good Works is much more inclined to hire individuals after they have been interns or volunteers; they know what they are getting into, and we know them.

For the founding leader, there is a tension between the wisdom of working oneself out of a job—in a sense being replaceable—and the reality that each member of the community is irreplaceable. Every leader places a unique imprint on the work, and founders often have a role that is difficult for another person to fill. I (Keith) see myself as Good Works' greatest asset and greatest liability.

Leadership Motifs

Another way of viewing some of the themes covered in this chapter is to see how they fit particular leadership motifs: leader as ship captain, archaeologist, orchestra conductor, and environmentalist. For me (Keith), environmentalist has been the best fit recently, but each captures some aspect of leadership concerns and dynamics.

Much like for **ship captains**, an important part of a ministry leader's role is to see and warn staff about what is ahead. Captains know where the ship is going, and a leader can lessen anxiety and hardship by anticipating the coming challenges. A related characteristic of leaders is foresight, a capacity to ask how a decision or choice might affect morale or expectations in the future. Just because a choice is most expedient now, it can still be a disaster if it leads to mistrust, disrespect, or hurt for people later. Leaders must think about the long-term impact of their actions and decisions while also attending to the immediate needs of the ministry. A test of leadership is the ability to navigate trends and changes in the community and the larger environment.

Like **archaeologists**, good leaders dig. They ask: "What is it that motivates people, that makes people want to carry on with a sense of devotion and loyalty? How can we keep them in the organization even when they don't want to continue in their particular jobs? How can we move people around or expand the vision of the organization? Can we listen to the passions of the people we love and trust, and carry their vision out rather than exclusively inviting them to join in our vision?" This involves digging deep and allows us to hold onto staff over the long term.

Good leaders also search for qualities in people that they do not see in themselves; helping them identify things they had not noticed and facilitating means by which they can activate or further that area of development. Leaders, then, help people clarify their callings and gifts. They invite people into new levels of growth and purpose with a mixture of challenge and grace, but they also need discernment to know when to ask for more and when to hold back. Leaders see, develop, and celebrate the potential of others; but to do so requires that the leaders themselves come to terms with where they derive their own sense of identity, fulfillment, and self-esteem.

Like **orchestra conductors**, leaders keep hold of the big picture and work (as far as it depends on them) toward the unity of the body of Christ. One of the things that has given me (Keith) the most pleasure is when I see person A and person B meet, and I watch the relationship develop, the goodness and the struggle with a volunteer and a staff person, or an elderly neighbor and an intern. I love being the conductor of the orchestra, seeing how the violins sound with the tubas, or how the different instruments play together. I'm not in those relationships, but I get to facilitate them. I notice as other leaders facilitate relationships as well. In a sense, leaders help to draw out the beauty of the entire community, in the way conductors draw out the sound of a whole orchestra, not just the individual parts.

Leaders as **environmentalists** attend to the ethos, space, and long-term viability of a community or project. I (Keith) want to create an environment that is life-giving for staff, where at the end of an average day, a person can say, "I really like what I do." Of course, there are really difficult days that involve hardship, sorrow, and sacrifice; but overall, the environment should be one that is good.

A good environment is also one that is life-giving for the people who are welcomed. In the early years of the Timothy House, Good Works learned about the importance of the environment—it needed to be safe, clean, and temporary but stable, in order for people to heal and move toward wholeness. Part of what creating a good environment means is that the staff developed the definitions of what behaviors were appropriate in the Timothy House and what were not. If someone comes in and jeopardizes a good environment—which does happen—it has to be addressed. For people who are struggling with homelessness and the factors that led to it, rules and the structures behind them make a place safe and secure.

Every institution has an environment, a climate. It is best to be intentional about cultivating it

Creating a good environment also involves nurturing good people. Staff members and volunteers need to be perceived as safe in the sense that others can count on their integrity, credibility, and predictability. When welcoming folks who have been harmed by betrayals and often by violence, it is particularly important that workers and the environment be safe and reliable.

In large events, it is also important for leaders to attend to shaping the environment. For example, between 90 and 150 people participate in Friday Night Life each week at Good Works. Leadership should know who is new and who is not, and should be able to monitor how things are going and assess whether the environment is contributing to people's growth or not. Sometimes we know what is best by seeing what is not helpful. But every institution has an environment, a climate. It is best to be intentional about cultivating it.

Conclusion

Recognizing the importance of creating life-giving environments means leaders must attend to what is happening in the community or organization and to how staff members and volunteers are reacting to what is happening. That means building a margin in one's life to be present to those experiences, learning to interpret them, and providing guidelines as needed. In the end, the hope is to create an environment that builds up the body of Christ.

Faithful leadership depends on the other commitments we have explored: worshiping God in community, practicing integrity, valuing and learning from different perspectives, and building life-giving friendships. As we turn to the concluding chapter, we consider more directly the formative power of good works, the significance of heroic communities and hospitality, and additional "holy tensions."

Prayer

*Lord, when you call, help each of us to say, "Here I am.
Send me." We want to live faithfully and to finish well. Create
in us clean hearts and renew a right spirit within us (Ps. 51).
Give us wisdom and discernment, caring and truthful friends,
good work and loving accountability in the arenas of ministry
to which you call us.
Amen.*

Questions for Reflection and Discussion

1. In what ways have you learned to handle (or seen handled well) these challenges or tensions in leadership:
    a. Taking individual situations *and* institutional needs seriously
    b. Being a good teacher *and* learner
    c. Expectations about sacrifice
    d. Building trust and trustworthiness
2. How has a commitment to accountability helped you respond to difficult people and various temptations?
3. In what ways have you seen power used well or poorly by people in leadership roles? What have you learned?
4. How has innovation been encouraged in your community? How have you handled concerns that the community stay true to its mission/vision (and avoid "drift") while embracing change or innovation?
5. What would it mean for you to finish well? Where have you seen good fruit come from long-term commitment to individuals or a community?
6. What leadership model best captures your leadership style or approach? Is there another motif that expresses it better? Why?

SIX

How Are Good Works Good?

Over the centuries, faithful followers of Jesus have tried to live out the relationship between their faith and their good works by emphasizing one or the other, seeing one as giving evidence for the other, or trying to hold them together. Living by faith and practicing good works in response to God's love, welcome, and commands to do good are at the heart of the story of the Good Works community. And yet, some of us still might wonder, just how are good works good?

We know that they are meant to be good for the recipients of our actions. If a stranger is in trouble, we render aid. If a friend is ill, we visit or bring a meal, and so on. And those persons are usually helped by our attention. Occasionally, of course, there are complications, but generally, people who are hungry, without shelter, lonely, or lost benefit from our efforts. People's lives are improved or changed. Through our good works, sometimes persons even discover their own beauty and potential and find healing and hope. Good works are acts of love, expressions of love for neighbor and God.

Good works are . . . a crucial avenue for formation in Christlikeness

But there are also important ways in which good works are formative for those who engage in them. That is why the community of Good Works gives people opportunities to be generous

143

and to help others. Good works are an aspect of discipleship, a crucial avenue for formation in Christlikeness. Good works are often viewed as acts of obedience and duty, which they are. But they are much more; they are following in the steps of Jesus, a central practice of the Christian life.

Our acts of love and generosity do not "save" us. Neither do they help us earn God's affection or attention; we already have that. They do help us become more like the one who has welcomed us, and they are powerful expressions of our faith, humanity, and identity. In Ephesians 2:8-10, we read that we were "created for good works." That helps us understand why we often feel good when we do good things. It is because we are most complete, most fulfilled, when we are being who we were meant to be. In doing good works, we actually live into that wholeness—at least sometimes.

A persistent surprise in the practice of good works is how much the person providing the help is transformed. The early church understood this, and certain writers throughout the centuries have described it. In God's economy, it seems that good works can be good for everyone. In the eighteenth century, John Wesley wrote that "works of mercy are a real means of grace." Of course, we hope that they bring grace to the recipient, but Wesley was referring to how they also affect the person who provides help. Done with the right spirit, good works can move us more deeply into holiness and a Christlike life. Wesley reminds us that care should be given with a sense of humility and inadequacy; we should be deeply convinced that we are not sufficient for the task. In his sermon "On Visiting the Sick," he explains how important it is that we recognize that we have "neither sufficient grace, nor sufficient understanding, to perform it in the most excellent manner." And as we come to understand this, it will convince us of the necessity of turning to God for help—crying out for the "whole spirit of humility, lest if pride steal into your heart, if you ascribe anything to yourself, while you strive to save others you destroy your own soul." Throughout our works of mercy, Wesley says, "let your heart wait upon him [God] for a continual supply of meekness and gentleness, of patience and long-suffering, that you may never be angry or discouraged at whatever treatment, rough or smooth, kind or unkind, you may meet with."[1]

Participation in good works can be revelatory. Sometimes the interactions reveal our mistaken assumptions, immaturity, pettiness, and fragility. They can challenge some of our simplistic answers and provoke more complicated but also more perceptive responses. And if we are embedded in a community that is committed to mutuality, forgiveness, and helping us process these experiences, we can mature in Christlikeness.

Not surprisingly, because every one of us is flawed, our efforts at good works sometimes go awry. Especially when our assistance is not offered in a spirit of humility and love, it can inadvertently or deliberately humiliate the very people we are trying to help. This is especially true when we assume that we are bringing all the resources, and the "needy" person is bringing only his or her need. If there is not a sense that both of us have gifts and both of us have needs, there is little opportunity for transformation in the encounter. Good works are good when there is mutuality.

Do we experience grace-filled mutuality in every relationship? Surely not. That's part of the sacrifice of service, the daily laying down of our lives for others. It is not a magic formula where all of us always benefit. But by grace, God often uses our experiences and sacrifices to expand our love, shape our character, extend our

1. John Wesley, Sermon 98: "On Visiting the Sick," in *The Works of John Wesley*, vol. 3 (Nashville: Abingdon, 1986), 389-90.

vision, clarify our kingdom commitments, and reveal our hidden sins. Not every time, but little by little, we are transformed.

In the mutuality—the give and take—of relationships, those who are willing can be changed. The person in need of a home gains a new sense of self and purpose as she and her children are given a place in community. A volunteer's perception is broadened by becoming friends with an elderly widower who has much wisdom to share but few contacts with young people. A staff member comes to understand vulnerability in a new way by working alongside another staff person who remembers well what it is like as a child to be unsure of where the next meal will come from.

The emphasis on good works in connection with building life-giving relationships of mutuality winds through Good Works' practices. As one person explained,

> We have many volunteers come to work alongside us as we build ramps, mow lawns, replace rotting floors, and plant gardens through Neighbors Helping Neighbors. We do these kinds of projects for people throughout the year, and the gratitude on the neighbor's face and in their words is very evident. This kind of help can be profound, and we are grateful for all the volunteers who accomplish these tasks. But that is not all that we are seeking to do. At the center of this initiative is the development of nurturing relationships with people who are often isolated due to age and disability. Many times, volunteers just *visit* while the project is taking place. And sometimes the person going to volunteer discovers that they are the neighbor who needed the help of a transforming relationship!

Good works are integral to the discipled life. One former staff member explained, "One of the most powerful things I experienced while working at the Timothy House was watching people who came to 'serve' really get it, and really start to understand how serving those in need is not an extra thing to check off your list, but a way of life—what following Jesus is all about."

The change may happen quickly or slowly, but either way, it can have far-reaching impact. The wife of a former staff member described their experience as a family and how they learned to be good neighbors.

My husband had just finished seminary, and we were considering all our options for ministry. We seemingly chose the one that made the least financial sense for a young family of six (we had four kids between the ages of three and nine). We moved to Athens, Ohio, and into the Good Works community. It made us rich in spirit!

We lived a few houses down from the Timothy House, so there were many opportunities to engage with residents who came and went from there. And every Friday, we all looked forward to "Friday Night Supper." Those nights were an opportunity for the young and old, the rich and poor, the highly educated and high school dropouts, the socially popular and socially awkward to mingle, share a meal, and create shared experiences. Our children thrived as they were befriended by people different from themselves.

Over the years of living near the Timothy House, I learned the importance of creating sacred space to welcome those I had invited and those who crashed in. Keith frequently talked about the importance of stewarding our personal time to include those without their own social network. As a result, loving our neighbors became a natural extension of loving life where God had placed us. That is how we met Patty.

We first encountered her at a Friday Night Supper and discovered she lived directly across the street from us. Every day at 4:00 p.m., after Patty's case worker left her home, Patty crossed the street to visit us. She had been deinstitutionalized from a mental health facility about a decade prior to our family moving into the neighborhood. Patty would enter our home and immediately turn down her hearing aid to adjust to our ruckus. As I was preparing for dinner, Patty watched cartoons with our kids or played "Connect Four" with our six-year-old daughter.

Patty would never leave until I would say, "Let me walk you home, Patty." That was usually around 10:00 p.m. Four or five nights a week for three years, she shared a meal with us. During that season of life, more than any other, I felt we embodied "the church."

Among those who volunteer at Good Works are a number who do not self-identify as followers of Jesus. Providing them with the opportunity to do good, to find fulfillment in transforming relationships, and to see the body of Christ at work also gives them a chance to discover aspects of God's kingdom and the church that they haven't necessarily experienced before. Good Works creates a platform for generosity—providing multiple environments and events that draw people into community, mission, and the family of Christ.

Participation in good works fills a need to be needed

When we have a chance to give, we become more of who we are, more of who we were meant to be. Participation in good works fills a need to be needed—and this is important for volunteers, staff, supporters, and those who receive assistance. Activities and events at Good Works are structured so that every person in need of help also gets to provide help. Initiatives like Neighbors Helping Neighbors and The Transformation Station are explicitly designed to facilitate this.

How Are Good Works Good?

In this book, we have shared what the community of Good Works has learned about good works over the years. We learned that without a foundation in Christ and in worship, our efforts are unsustainable, that loving God and loving neighbors are wound together in rich and life-giving ways, and that good works come out of our belovedness and are a way of living out that belovedness. We discovered that integrity and trust are more essential than good programs in helping others, and that to offer help in ways that are good requires a bigger and fuller perspective than what any single individual ever has. We learned that good works done in community are a part of being and building the body of Christ, doing Jesus's work of healing and wholeness in the world.

Heroic Communities

Most of us have heroes. Whether action figures or real people, they challenge and inspire us and often help us want to be better than we are. They are usually individuals who make a significant difference in the lives of others. But we don't often think about heroic communities—communities that make a difference, communities that intentionally make "little moves against destructiveness."[2] Their "moves" are usually less dramatic than what we see in a single heroic figure, and they often work slowly over time, chipping away at misery, injustice, and loneliness.

Heroic communities provide a context for people to be generous and courageous; they provide the structure, environment, and necessary support for members to be able to do this over

2. Philip Hallie, *Lest Innocent Blood Be Shed* (New York: Harper & Row, 1979), 85.

the long term. Could our communities or congregations be described as heroic? Where are the groups of people that make us say: "Wow, could we ever be like that?"

Heroic communities are "contrast-societies,"[3] created by people who intentionally share life together, live out of specific shared values, and intentionally organize to "love our neighbors as ourselves." Heroic communities look different from their surrounding society and are often characterized by deep concern for, and commitment to, those who are most vulnerable.

Heroic communities invite us and provoke us to be better—to live more faithfully and courageously, to walk more closely with the Lord of life. They provoke us by creating beauty amid brokenness. Their life-giving message is demonstrated by the love they provide and explained in the good news they proclaim.

Are heroic communities made up of superhero figures? Not usually—mostly they are inhabited by people who are generous, faithful, willing to make sacrifices, and able to laugh at themselves and learn from their mistakes. But in such communities, individuals can be courageous and are more able to deal with adversity. Good Works doesn't fit the typical assumptions about dramatic individual heroism or idealized community, but by its fidelity, mutuality, and tenacity, the community challenges us to deeper commitments and more generous lifestyles.

Ruined by Hospitality?

In this book, I (Christine) have described the Good Works community as a demonstration plot, a heroic community, and a contrast society. The description that is most personal to me,

3. Gerhard Lohfink, *Jesus and Community* (Philadelphia: Fortress, 1984), 179–80.

however, is that it is a community of hospitality. After more than thirty years of researching, writing, and teaching about Christian hospitality, I can say that Good Works is among the most powerful embodiments of the practice of hospitality I have encountered. They have lived what I have written and taught. And what I have written and taught is much wiser and truer because of what I have learned from them.

We had a rocky start. When I was doing research for my book *Making Room*, I went to Good Works for the first time to interview Keith, the staff, and the residents. I knew enough about Good Works to be quite sure that it fit the criteria I had developed in identifying communities of hospitality from whom I was eager to learn. Good Works had stood the test of time; they consistently described their work as offering welcome, making room, providing a home or open door for strangers; they explicitly identified their life and ministry with biblical texts important to the hospitality tradition; and guests and host ate together regularly at the same table and shared life with people who in some way had been strangers. So, when I started interviewing Keith, I asked him, "Would you describe your ministry as offering hospitality to strangers?" He responded, "No, not really." At that point, I was both startled and dismayed, but his follow-up comment was very illuminating. For him, the term *hospitality* meant "entertaining family and friends," and Good Works "welcome[s] needy strangers into a home environment" and "give[s] them a safe place."[4]

As Keith and I talked, and as I shared research with him that broadened his definition of hospitality, he agreed that what they were doing was indeed "hospitality." Happily, I learned

Heroic communities invite us and provoke us to be better

---

4. Christine D. Pohl, *Making Room: Recovering Hospitality as a Christian Tradition* (Grand Rapids: Eerdmans, 1999), 3.

much about hospitality from the Good Works community, and the Good Works community learned, from some of the academic and historical research I'd done, a language and tradition that made sense of their deepest commitments and most significant practices.

Keith explains that seeing themselves as part of a Christian tradition of hospitality shifted the paradigm of Good Works and reshaped how they viewed their mission. New vocabulary became a door to seeing things differently, to noticing practices they would later attach to a vision of hospitality. Almost everything they did fit into the category of hospitality, and understandings of hospitality became weightier. And Good Works became a living embodiment of hospitality for me. It was true collaboration.

But the story of collaboration and mutuality didn't end there. A few years later when I was working on a project about practices that build and destroy community, Keith was an important participant in the project meetings. Like the other individuals in the group, he brought wisdom from the community in which he was rooted. The project identified four central practices that build and sustain community: gratitude, promise making and keeping, truthfulness, and hospitality. The book, *Living into Community*, emerged from conversations with these pastors and community leaders.[5] However, the book was not the only fruit of our time together. Like several of the other participants, Keith took the opportunity to make these four practices explicitly central to community life. Practices that had emerged from the experience of building and sustaining communities became more explicit in the book and then were more deliberately embodied in those same communities. At Good Works, the four

5. Christine D. Pohl, *Living into Community: Cultivating Practices That Sustain Us* (Grand Rapids: Eerdmans, 2012).

practices became "studs in the wall" of their life together,[6] and that emphasis is evident in the chapters of this book.

This lengthy description of our fruitful relationship is an effort to describe how a community can embody concepts and commitments without necessarily naming them. When they are identified and given a historical, theological, or moral context, and the community begins to see itself as part of a larger tradition, that community also lives into and furthers the tradition. It expands reflection by bringing additional sets of questions and insights that arise from its particular time and context.

The hospitality tradition captures the mutuality that has been so important to Good Works over the decades. One former intern and volunteer said that she particularly valued the experience of creating a welcoming setting that offers dignity by blurring boundaries between "insiders" or experts and "outsiders." It creates an environment in which people have a chance to be generous, to share their gifts and to have them received with gratitude.

Good works, if they are personal and mutually respectful, almost always involve hospitality

Here's a description of how hospitality worked for one newly married couple who served at Good Works as the Hannah House managers.[7]

> We had only an inkling of what we were signing up for. What we found was a big house in various states of repair and disrepair. We found long hours staffing the house during the days, evenings, and weekends. But most of all we found people: residents working through the challenges of long-term homelessness, other staff members who became our

6. See http://good-works.net/going-deeper.
7. The Hannah House is located on Good Works' Luhrig Road property and serves multiple functions. See the appendix for further details.

local body of Christ, interns coming to follow Jesus in their life and work, and guests of all kinds, from friends to visitors to large groups coming to serve with the ministry. We shared daily meals. We talked with people with beautiful souls from every walk of life. . . . It was all very fruitful and all very stressful.

Several years later, we were in a new state with new children trying to fit into a new place. It was not going so well, and we sought God for wisdom about our nagging sense of loss and confusion. Then we realized that Good Works had ruined us—ruined us in so many good ways. It ruined our ability to tolerate incomplete and one-sided expressions of the gospel. It ruined our habit of turning a blind eye to the presence of Jesus in the vulnerable people around us. It ruined us for shallow Christian relationships. . . . It ruined us for comfortable and complacent living. . . . Life has never been the same since Good Works ruined us, and for that we will be eternally grateful.

Good works, if they are personal and mutually respectful, almost always involve hospitality. Whether it is a staff member and a person who is homeless sharing life stories over coffee and muffins, or an elderly widow and volunteers resting on her porch sharing her sweet tea and peanut butter sandwiches, each person has the opportunity to do good works and practice hospitality. Hospitality is often expressed in small acts of respect and generosity. It doesn't necessarily call attention to itself unless it is a response very different from what is being offered by the larger community. So when someone who is usually overlooked is welcomed into a community, it can be a significant statement of a different way of valuing persons. When that is practiced over time and involves significant sacrifice or courage, we might even call it heroic.

How Are Good Works Good?

Holy Tensions

One of the reasons that hospitality and good works more generally are so generative and transforming is that within their practice are held many dynamic tensions. Because they are often also recognized in Scripture, we can consider them "holy" tensions. To engage well in good works and to practice hospitality faithfully involve learning how to navigate these tensions. But navigation is often messy and difficult, because we are all flawed, and because the commitments themselves pull us in different directions and play out differently in different contexts. Our tendency is to focus on one or the other, but most of the time, if only one of the pair is emphasized or valued, much is lost.

Many of the tensions have been identified and discussed in the earlier chapters of the book as they emerged in the life of the Good Works community. A few that were noted include loving God and loving our neighbors, which sometimes draw us in different directions, but they are not at odds, and, as they are held together, they capture the core of what we were created for. Communities struggle with maintaining a strong connection between worship or intimacy with God and work for justice and care. But those commitments are strongly held together in the prophets of the Old Testament, in the life of Jesus, and in the practices of the early church. Emphases on demonstration (living out our faith) and proclamation (describing and explaining it in words) are sometimes seen as alternatives, but they are both crucial to embodying the good news of Jesus.

Ministry and mission under challenging circumstances remind us again and again that human beings are sinful and frail, but also beloved and beautiful. As we recognize this complicated mixture of features, we are better able to help and to be helped. As has been evident in the Good Works community, it is difficult

yet essential to find ways to offer assistance and build friendships at the same time. These forms of relationship are not held
together in most social service or social ministry settings, nor
in our personal lives, and yet together they offer life-changing
experiences.

In providing various forms of help, we long for the person's
immediate healing, complete restoration, and full salvation, and
yet we recognize that much of the change comes in small, incremental steps over time. Rarely instan-
taneous, transformation requires the
slow building of trust and fidelity. We
want to help everyone who needs help,
but we encounter limits as individuals
and communities. We struggle and
grieve when we come up against the
limits, and yet we press on, remember-
ing that this too is a form of worship. We trust that we are making a difference for some people, even as we are sometimes desperate. Living in the tensions prompts humility, honesty, and
dependence on God.

We long for the person's
immediate healing, complete
restoration, and full salvation,
and yet we recognize that much
of the change comes in small,
incremental steps over time

When we have worked to create a life-giving community,
we encounter other tensions. We want to maintain the identity
and commitments of the community and at the same time offer
welcome to strangers. That means bumping up against the edges
of identity and difference and learning what parts of our identity are crucial and fundamental to who we are, and what parts
should be modified to welcome people who are different from us
in significant ways. This is a tension that is crucial to providing
environments that are both stable and allow for growth.

Life at Good Works, lives of good works, receiving welcome
and offering hospitality, loving and being loved, following Jesus and being his body—these are all both challenging and life-

giving. The words of a former staff member at Good Works bring our account to a close:

> I came to Good Works because I longed to see the church in action. I stayed at Good Works because I was so grateful to be welcomed, known, and loved. I grew at Good Works in learning to love others, living in Christian community, and welcoming people from all walks of life into my own life. I remember Good Works for helping me understand what the good news of Jesus looks like when it is embodied in real life—flawed, forgiving, encouraging, and deeply loving people.

Prayer

Thank you, Lord, for creating us, calling us, and equipping us
for good works. We pray for your forgiveness, guidance,
wisdom, and grace as we seek to live out what we read
in Ephesians 2:10: that we are your "workmanship, created
in Christ Jesus to do good works" (NIV).
Amen.

Questions for Reflection and Discussion

1. How have you been changed by experiences of volunteering?
2. How have your understandings of discipleship been expanded by thinking more about the ways good works are good for everyone?
3. Share an experience when you thought you were helping and you discovered that you were really the one being helped.

4. Have there been times you were disappointed by the results of your good works? Why?

5. Have you encountered a heroic community? What was it like? In what ways would you describe your church or community as heroic?

6. How do you understand the role of hospitality in the Christian life? Reflect on the way offering and receiving welcome has been important in your experience.

7. What "holy" tensions have you experienced in your life, church, or community? How have you navigated them?

8. In what ways has the story of Good Works affected the way you think about your life, church, friendships, or calling?

The Settings for Good Works'
Mission and Ministry

Four commitments, rooted in our philosophy of ministry, guide Good Works' efforts in shaping contexts for healing and wholeness.[1] First, we emphasize building relationships rather than programs. Every program and structure is designed to support and facilitate the deepening of relationships. Second, building and maintaining trust is the focus of these relationships, and in every context, we ask: *What are we doing here that builds or diminishes trust?* Third, each context meets a "felt need."[2] It might be a need for shelter, food, a car, companionship, or the need to be needed. And fourth, in every context, we are looking for ways a *recipient* can move toward being a *participant*. This means we are looking for an identity change: the person is no longer "that homeless guy"; he is Bill with gifts that can contribute to the community.

Good Works has also made a commitment to the well-being of our larger neighborhoods, recognizing that our neighbors live

---

1. See "Vision of Hope," http://good-works.net/wp-content/uploads /PDF%20Documents/Vision-of-Hope.pdf.

2. John Perkins, *Beyond Charity: The Call to Christian Community Development* (Grand Rapids: Baker, 1993), 30–38.

around us all year long. Annually, we welcome into our neighborhood between one hundred and two hundred strangers who stay at the Timothy House, and another three hundred to four hundred overnight guests at our Luhrig Road property. We want to make sure we are sensitive to the concerns of our immediate neighbors with the goal of building trust and having good communication. We keep our property clean and attractive at all times and provide regular ways for our neighbors to come in and meet our staff. We try to be proactive because we believe we should be a community that is a good for everyone, and a witness to the people where we live. Loving our neighbors begins in our neighborhood.

Shared meals are an important and consistent feature of life at Good Works. Meals occur regularly at the Timothy House, Hannah House, Friday Night Life, and the Summer Lunch program. A long-time staff member describes mealtimes as nearly sacred because they combine friendship, food, and gratitude in such life-giving ways. By bringing together residents, staff, volunteers, visitors, and guests for the meal, conversation, and clean-up, friendships are formed, and social differences are often transcended.

Below are brief descriptions of the contexts Good Works has developed. Many more details are available on the website: goodworks.net.

The Timothy House

The Timothy House is located within the city of Athens and provides temporary housing for men, women, and children who have lost their homes. As noted earlier, it is the only shelter facility in eight counties, but it is far more than a standard shelter. Good Works' objective for the Timothy House is to provide a safe, clean, stable, and comfortable place for people while they receive assistance in identifying and addressing underlying problems that led to their current circumstances. Residents prepare and eat meals with staff members and volunteers. The Timothy House is the setting where relationships often begin, and where trust is initially built. The house can host fifteen people at a time; their length of stay varies and is tied to a set of criteria developed by the community years ago. The Timothy House's structure depends on approximately forty to fifty regular volunteers who come alongside the staff to enrich and strengthen community life. A new building is being constructed that will provide additional housing, especially for those with mobility limitations and families. By December 2020, the Timothy House had provided more than 125,000 nights of shelter since we started keeping statistics in 1984.

Friday Night Life

Friday Night Life (FNL) began in 1993 when we invited former Timothy House residents who had found stable housing to come back on Friday evenings to share a meal and maintain connections with our community. Since then, the gathering has expanded to include others facing poverty or longing for friendship. Now we welcome current and former residents of the Timothy House, community members, seniors, university students, teenagers, children, volunteers, interns, and staff. Each week, a different church or community organization provides the food for the meal, and between 90 and 150 people participate. This is another way that relationships are built and reinforced in the community. The time together involves a sit-down, family-style supper and a variety of activities, including: volleyball, basketball, poetry, art, Bible study, live music, health education, special presentations, and clean-up. A special kids club is held for those ages 4–17. From April to September, the gathering is held at the Good Works' Luhrig Road property, and from October to March it is held at The Plains United Methodist Church.

Friday Night Life Friendship

Within the Friday Night Life gathering, some individuals make a commitment to be *with* others in an intentional way during the evening. We encourage volunteers to seek out individuals who seem to be less connected to other people and to intentionally visit with them and get to know them. These volunteers commit to participating for three hours each Friday night for three months, but many stay much longer.

Transformation Station

Created in 2004 when we were simultaneously looking for ways to assist people struggling with poverty and provide opportunities that would allow them to give back to others, the Transformation Station is based on an economy of time rather than money. Through various donations to Good Works, we are able to provide much-needed items for people, particularly automobiles, appliances, bicycles, and food. This approach is oriented to people facing long-term problems, not those in crisis who need to be helped quickly and directly. The Transformation Station opens up a "third way" for people to obtain needed resources—not by buying things, or by our giving them away, but by serving others. By volunteering their time and using their skills and abilities to help other people, participants in the Transformation Station earn points they can "cash in" to obtain something they need. It is a form of sweat equity and can involve, among other things, helping with home repair, property and lawn maintenance, construction, meal preparation, small engine repair, and mailings. Paired with staff members and other volunteers, individuals do physical work alongside others and trade their "needy" person identity for that of volunteer or helper. We can often see the transformation. In sharing life and lunch together, trust is built along with mutual respect. Cars are especially needed because transportation is so important in rural areas, and the ability to obtain a car and learn how to maintain it is a huge benefit. At the time of this writing, Good Works had provided 185 cars. We estimate that for each family or individual who receives a vehicle through the Transformation Station, there is a direct impact on as many as four other families here in rural Ohio.

Neighbors Helping Neighbors

As noted above, participants in the Transformation Station who are in need of resources are able to become volunteers who help others. They work alongside volunteers from local organizations and from churches whose members travel from all over the United States to assist our neighbors in Athens County, spend time with them, and do labor-intensive projects at their homes. Each year, nearly four hundred volunteers participate in assisting older adults and people with disabilities who find it difficult to care for their own homes.

Luhrig Road Property

Various buildings, centers, and projects are located on our thirty-five-acre rural property. The Hannah House is used for housing interns, visiting work groups called Work Retreats, and, occasionally, persons moving out of homelessness who need extra time to transition to independent living. The Luhrig Road property is also the site of Good Works' administrative offices, a bed and breakfast business, the Transformation Station, two miles of hiking trails, and the Carter Cabin for individual retreats. Friday Night Life is held there in the warmer months.

Work Retreats

Through our Work Retreats, Good Works provides a structure so that outside groups can serve in the broader Athens community. While Work Retreat groups engage in helping our neighbors in need, these experiences are also oriented to creating opportunities to form mutual relationships among those we bring together. We also invite the groups to worship alongside our community throughout their visit. In an average year, Good Works hosts approximately twenty-five to thirty-five different groups from around the United States who stay for a weekend or a week-long service experience.

Agricultural Initiatives and Good Works Gardens

Diabetes and obesity are at dangerously high levels in rural Appalachia, and those who struggle with poverty often have limited access to fresh, nutritious, and low-cost food. Along with a greenhouse and large garden on the Luhrig Road property, Good Works staff and volunteers help to start and maintain gardens at the homes of friends who are widowed or experiencing disability. During the summer, Good Works offers an agricultural internship for local teens. Three of the Good Works Internship programs—the Appalachian Immersion Internship, Summer Service Internship, and the Teen Agricultural Internship—provide individuals to work with the Good Works Gardens.

Internships

The Appalachian Internship Program is a full-time internship for individuals who want to spend three, six, nine, or twelve months in ministry with Good Works.

The Hannah House Internship is a part-time internship for those who serve with Good Works while living with people who have been homeless or struggling with other life-controlling issues.

The Summer Service Internship is an intensive nine-week experience working with our visiting Work Retreat groups during the summer.

The Week of Service Internship is an opportunity for anyone, ages sixteen or older, to come for one week in order to serve alongside the staff and experience the community.

The Teen Agricultural Internship is designed for local teens from several high schools in rural Athens County to experience a seven-week educational internship in growing food.

The Kingdom Internship is a seven-week summer discipleship experience designed for teens from local congregations who want to grow deeper in their relationship with Christ by learning to love and serve others.

Life in Transition

For men and women who have been caught in the revolving door of homelessness, Good Works provides a more extended opportunity for them to work on their long-term issues in a supportive Christian community at the Hannah House. With interns who live at the Hannah House for six to twelve months, we have developed a mentoring program to help people establish healthy and holy habits in the context of Christian community.

Life Together

Life Together is a worshiping community established through Good Works that meets Sunday evenings on the Luhrig Road property. Because of a growing desire to bring together people from different arenas of our ministry and Christians from different traditions, Life Together was formed in 2016 with a vision to create a place of welcome and spiritual growth. Gatherings include a time of worship and a shared meal.

Senior Friends

Seniors who would like visitors regularly are paired with area volunteers who want to learn and grow from their relationship with older persons who are widows, widowers, home-bound, or people with physical disabilities. Volunteers agree to visit twice a month for two to three hours with the hope of building new friendships.

Sign of HOPE

Sign of HOPE is the name we have chosen to describe our newest initiative. This house, being built across the street from the Timothy House on the west side of Athens, will provide additional space for people who cannot be accommodated at the Timothy House. Our new building will be especially helpful to families and people with mobility limitations.

Spiritual Formation Retreats

For several years, Good Works has been hosting and leading spiritual formation experiences for small groups. These have taken several forms, which make use of the beautiful outdoor environment of the Luhrig Road property.

Summer Kids Discovery Club

For many years, Good Works has provided a summer camp (Summer Discovery Club) for children grades K-6. Kids meet from 9:00 a.m. to 1:00 p.m. four to five days a week for seven weeks. We intentionally include children from families who struggle with poverty and those from families who do not.

Summer Lunch Program

In this initiative, volunteers meet immediate food needs of adults and children during the summer by providing a daily nutritious meal. This intergenerational lunch has been the site for forming many new friendships and connections among individuals, businesses, and organizations who provide the food. We enjoy welcoming parents and grandparents to share a meal together with their children, grandchildren, and neighbors.

Afterword

We completed this book during the COVID-19 pandemic. Not surprisingly, it is hard to anticipate the long-term impact of this crisis on the Good Works community. Some activities have been interrupted or rearranged, although the overall focus has remained unchanged. Good Works already had many practices in place to move forward despite risks and restrictions. While, as a community, we have asked what hospitality and mission should look like in the midst of a pandemic, we have not asked whether we should offer hospitality or continue our work. As always, we pray, "Lord, what are the innovations and initiatives you desire that will embody the gospel for our time and community?"

Index

accountability: integrity and, 45–48; in leadership, 46, 47, 122, 127–29; ownership, autonomy and, 47, 128; perspective and, 80–81; for recipients of help, 98, 99; in relationships, 100–102; types of, 45

Achan, 41, 41n5

adversity, 62, 120

affirmation, 23–24, 125

agricultural initiatives, 164–65

Appalachian Immersion Internship, 165

appreciation, need for, 24, 100

archaeologist motif, 138

Athens County (Ohio), 3, 163

authority, 128, 130

autonomy, 47, 128

belovedness, 20–23

body of Christ: experienced through service, 6, 148; integration into, 8, 109, 110; interaction within, 22, 23, 38–39; leadership in, 138. *See also* church

bottom-up accountability, 45

boundaries, 44, 79, 100–102

calling *vs.* concern, 62–63

Carter Cabin, 105, 164

Central Appalachia, 3

character, 120. *See also* integrity

children, fatherless, 25, 82, 83, 99, 106

church: integrity in, 35–36; relationships in, 6, 89; serving vulnerable people through, 74–76, 105–8; worship and, 14. *See also* body of Christ

class barriers, 74, 94–95

"clear" practice, 48–50

Coleman, Robert, 62, 136n3

common ground, discovering, 76–77

community: belovedness in,

90; gratitude and affirmation as, 23–24; Great Commandment and, 18–20; intimacy with Christ as, 30–32; justice and, 26–30, 155; kingdom of God and, 24–26; location of, 15, 16; relationships and, 18, 38, 40–41, 96; service as, 14, 15, 16, 19–20, 31; service transformed by, 17–18, 25, 156; as spiritual discipline, 104–5; truthfulness and, 37–38

woundedness: among staff and volunteers, 80, 123–24; of people without homes, 69, 77–79; recognizing and addressing, 47, 80, 104, 123–24